The minimum you need to know about:

MySQL

CONTENTS

Introduction

My journey with databases began over a decade ago, in 2013, when I was just starting to explore the world of data management. Since then, I've had the privilege of working with MySQL and other database management systems (DBMS) across a range of industries, from small, agile startups to large corporations, including major banks, insurance companies, and, most recently, the private energy sector. This experience has allowed me to see firsthand how MySQL adapts to different needs, from the fast-paced development cycles of tech startups to the stringent demands of enterprise-level applications.

In the early days, working with startups, I quickly learned the value of speed, agility, and scalability. In these environments, MySQL proved to be a versatile tool, offering the perfect balance of simplicity and power. With its open-source nature, it was a go-to choice for developers who needed to get products off the ground quickly, iterate fast, and scale as user demand grew. MySQL's flexibility and ease of use were game-changers, allowing me and my teams to focus on building applications without getting bogged down by overly complex setups.

As I moved on to larger organizations, including some of the biggest banks and insurance companies, the game changed. These environments introduced new challenges: massive volumes of data, strict security requirements, compliance standards, and the need for high availability and performance optimization. Here, MySQL's robustness shone through, showing that it wasn't just a tool for startups but a reliable

DBMS that could handle the heavy lifting required by enterprise-level systems. From optimizing complex queries to designing resilient architectures, my work taught me how to harness the full potential of MySQL, ensuring data integrity and performance even under the most demanding conditions.

Now, in the private energy sector, I face yet another set of unique challenges. This field requires not only precise data management but also adherence to regulatory standards, which demand a deep understanding of data processing and optimization.

MySQL has once again proven to be a trustworthy ally, capable of adapting to these new requirements while continuing to deliver high performance and reliability. It's this adaptability across different sectors that makes MySQL such a valuable skill to master.

Over the years, I've learned that mastering MySQL is not just about understanding how to write SQL queries or manage databases. It's about understanding how to use data as a tool to drive business outcomes, whether it's enhancing customer experiences, optimizing internal processes, or making data-driven decisions. This book is a reflection of that understanding, and it aims to equip you with practical knowledge and real-world insights that I've gathered throughout my career.

But my mission to share knowledge doesn't end here. I'm also passionate about educating and inspiring others to learn about databases, programming, and technology in general. That's why I've created a YouTube channel, where I offer full, free courses on various tech topics, including MySQL.

The channel is a space for learners of all levels, where I break down complex concepts into simple, digestible lessons, making it easier for anyone to understand and apply them.

The MySQL course on my channel is designed to complement this book, offering practical demonstrations and hands-on exercises that build on the concepts we'll explore here.

In the same way, this book serves as a deeper companion to the video lessons, providing detailed explanations, examples, and insights that you can refer back to whenever needed.

Together, they form a complete learning experience.

I invite you to join me on YouTube at youtube.com/@4rtisn, where you can not only reinforce what you learn in this book but also engage with a community of fellow learners, ask questions, and deepen your understanding of MySQL.

As you immerse yourself in the world of technology, there's a chance you might fall into the same trap I once did—becoming so engrossed in learning and perfecting your skills that you lose sight of everything else.

In the pursuit of mastering new languages, frameworks, and coding techniques, I found myself spending countless hours in front of a screen, neglecting my physical and mental health. This relentless focus, while beneficial in some ways, led to a sedentary lifestyle, increased stress, and a feeling of burnout.

Over time, I realized that true success in tech isn't just about what you can build or code; it's about finding balance, maintaining your well-being, and nurturing a life outside the digital realm. That's why I also share my journey of rediscovery, my hobbies, and what I call "side quests" on Instagram. By following me at **@4rtisn**, you'll get a glimpse of my life beyond the keyboard—whether it's engaging in physical activities, exploring new places, or simply taking time to disconnect and recharge.

I invite you to join me there, not just to see another side of who I am, but to remind yourself of the importance of stepping away from the screen now and then. Let my experiences be a guide to finding your own balance, so that your passion for technology becomes a part of a fulfilling and healthy lifestyle, rather than something that consumes you. Follow me at instagram.com/4rtisn, and let's navigate this journey together.

In this book, I will take you through the essentials of MySQL, starting from the basics and gradually progressing to more advanced concepts. Whether you're a beginner just getting started or an experienced developer looking to refine your skills, this book has something for you. You'll learn how to install and configure MySQL, design efficient databases, write complex queries, optimize performance, and much more. But beyond the technical knowledge, I hope to share some of the lessons I've learned along the way—lessons that go beyond code, about the importance of curiosity, adaptability, and continuous learning.

Thank you for picking up this book. I'm excited to share my journey with you, and I hope it inspires you to master MySQL and explore the incredible potential of data management. Let's get started!

Understanding Data Types

When diving into MySQL, one of the foundational concepts that every developer must grasp is the notion of data types. Imagine setting out on a journey, where the first step is to understand the different types of data you'll encounter along the way. This understanding forms the bedrock of effective database design and management.

As I began my exploration of MySQL, I quickly realized that data types are not merely technical specifications; they are the language through which the database communicates. Each type serves a specific purpose, influencing how data is stored, processed, and retrieved. This realization felt like unlocking a new level of insight.

In MySQL, data types are categorized primarily into three groups: numeric, string, and date/time types. Each category plays a crucial role in how we interact with our data. Numeric data types, for instance, are essential for performing calculations. As I navigated through the different numeric types—ranging from TINYINT for small numbers to BIGINT for larger integers—I appreciated the nuance in their storage requirements and performance implications. Choosing the right numeric type can optimize both memory usage and processing speed, which are critical for the performance of any application.

Then, there are string data types. These types allow us to store text, but they come in various forms, each designed for specific use cases. I found myself pondering the difference between CHAR and VARCHAR, realizing that while CHAR is fixed-length and can be useful for storing data of a consistent size, VARCHAR is more flexible, adapting to the actual length of the string. This flexibility can save space, particularly in large databases where many entries are shorter than the maximum length.

As I delved deeper, I encountered the date and time data types. Understanding these was pivotal, especially as I began to build applications that required tracking events over time. The distinction between DATETIME, TIMESTAMP, and DATE became clear, and I appreciated how each type served its purpose in maintaining temporal data. The nuances of handling time zones and the implications of using TIMESTAMP for automatic updates sparked a curiosity about how data is not just static but dynamic and responsive.

Throughout this journey, the importance of choosing the correct data type became increasingly apparent. I realized that selecting a data type is akin to laying the groundwork for a sturdy building; if the foundation is not solid, everything built on top is at risk. I began to appreciate the impact of data integrity and how the right data types help enforce constraints, preventing invalid data entries.

One day, while optimizing a large database, I took a moment to reflect on my past mistakes—using larger data types than necessary and experiencing performance hits as a result. I learned to ask myself critical questions: "Do I really need a BIGINT here, or would a SMALLINT suffice?" This shift in perspective helped me become a more thoughtful developer, one who considered the implications of every decision.

As I continued to refine my understanding, I started implementing best practices in my projects. I became vigilant about choosing the smallest possible data type for each field, ensuring that my databases were not only efficient but also easy to maintain. I discovered the power of normalization, using appropriate data types to reduce redundancy and enhance data integrity across related tables.

This exploration of MySQL data types opened my eyes to the art of database design. I learned that it's not just about storing data; it's about doing so in a way that maximizes performance, ensures accuracy, and provides clarity. Each time I designed a new database schema, I felt a renewed sense of purpose, equipped with the knowledge to make informed decisions that would lay the foundation for robust applications.

In summary, understanding data types in MySQL is a critical stepping stone in any developer's journey. It shapes how we think about data, influences our design choices, and ultimately determines the effectiveness of our applications. With each line of code, I carry forward the lessons learned about data types, forever shaping the way I approach database management and application development.

Installing MySQL

As I embarked on my journey to master MySQL, one of the first crucial steps was the installation process. It felt like preparing for a grand adventure, laying the groundwork for the knowledge and skills I was eager to acquire. The anticipation was palpable, knowing that a robust database system would soon be at my fingertips, ready to help me manage and manipulate data effectively.

To begin this process, I first needed to decide which environment I would use to install MySQL. My choices ranged from Windows to macOS and various Linux distributions. Each platform had its unique quirks, but I was determined to find the best path for my needs. After some research, I opted for Windows, as it was the system I was most familiar with at the time.

The official MySQL website became my go-to resource. I navigated through the various versions available and selected the latest stable release, feeling a sense of excitement with each click. Downloading the MySQL Installer was a straightforward process, but it carried a sense of promise— this would be the tool that would open up new possibilities for data management.

Once the installer was downloaded, I double-clicked the file, and the installation wizard launched. It felt like entering a new realm, where I would set the stage for my MySQL database. The wizard presented me with several configuration options, and I took my time to carefully read through each one. This was not just a formality; I understood that these choices would shape how MySQL would function on my machine.

I was presented with the option to choose a server type. The default selection, the "Developer Default," was tempting, as it promised a full installation of MySQL Server along with various tools that would aid in development. I selected it, excited at the prospect of having everything I needed at my fingertips.

As the installation progressed, I watched the progress bar with eager anticipation. With each step completed, I imagined the powerful database system coming to life, ready to assist me in managing data like never before. Finally, the installation wizard prompted me to configure the MySQL Server instance. This included choosing a server configuration type—development, production, or custom. I opted for the development configuration, as it suited my current learning needs.

Next came the moment of truth: setting the root password. I understood the importance of this step, as the root user would have full access to the database. I chose a strong password, one that would keep my database secure yet memorable enough for me to recall easily. It was an empowering moment, as I realized I was taking charge of my database environment.

With the basic configuration complete, I moved on to setting up MySQL as a Windows service. This option appealed to me because it would allow the server to start automatically whenever I booted my computer. I selected this option, ensuring that my database would always be ready for use without requiring manual intervention.

Once the installation and configuration were complete, I reached the final stage—launching MySQL Workbench. This graphical interface was like a dashboard to my database, offering a user-friendly way to interact with MySQL. As the Workbench opened, I felt a surge of excitement and possibility. I was finally ready to explore, create, and manipulate databases!

After a successful connection to my MySQL Server, I was greeted with a clean interface that displayed various options for managing databases. I took a moment to familiarize myself with the layout, exploring the query editor and the visual design tools. The power to create and manage databases was now in my hands, and the possibilities felt endless.

As I began my first few queries, the satisfaction of successfully interacting with the database was overwhelming. I created my first database, defined tables, and even inserted some initial data. Each successful operation reaffirmed that my installation journey had been worthwhile.

Looking back, I realized that installing MySQL was more than just setting up software on my computer; it was the beginning of a new chapter in my development journey. The steps I took to configure and optimize my installation laid a solid foundation for my future work with databases. With MySQL now at my disposal, I felt empowered to explore the intricacies of data management, ready to tackle challenges and seize opportunities that lay ahead.

In retrospect, the installation process was not merely a technical task but a vital rite of passage that connected me to the world of data. It instilled in me a sense of responsibility and curiosity, pushing me to delve deeper into MySQL's capabilities. With each new query I executed and each database I created, I knew I was on the path to mastering a powerful tool that would enrich my skills as a developer and data enthusiast.

Using MySQL Workbench

With MySQL successfully installed on my system, I was eager to delve into the next phase of my database journey: mastering MySQL Workbench. This powerful graphical interface promised to make interacting with MySQL not just efficient but also intuitive. As I launched the application for the first time, a sense of anticipation bubbled within me—this was where my data management skills would truly begin to flourish.

Upon opening MySQL Workbench, I was greeted by a clean and organized layout. The main dashboard displayed options for managing connections, creating new models, and performing queries. I quickly connected to my MySQL server, entering the root password I had established during the installation. As the connection was established, I felt a rush of excitement—this was my portal to the world of databases.

The first feature that caught my attention was the **Schema Navigator** on the left side of the window. This panel provided an overview of all the databases I had created. I found it incredibly convenient to visualize my databases and their structures in one place. As I clicked through my schemas, I realized how easy it was to manage tables, views, and stored procedures directly from this interface.

One of the standout features of MySQL Workbench was the **SQL Editor**. This is where the magic truly happened. I could type and execute SQL queries with ease. The editor's syntax highlighting helped me spot errors quickly, and the autocomplete feature felt like having a helpful companion guiding me through the SQL landscape. I began by creating my first table using a simple CREATE TABLE statement. As I crafted the SQL syntax, I marveled at how seamlessly the editor transformed my thoughts into actionable commands.

Executing queries became a thrilling experience. I typed out SELECT * FROM my_table; and pressed the execute button, holding my breath in anticipation. The results populated in the results grid below, and I felt a rush of accomplishment. I was no longer a passive observer; I was actively engaging with my data, pulling insights and information from my newly created tables.

With time, I began to explore more advanced features of MySQL Workbench. The **Data Modeling** tool allowed me to design complex database schemas visually. I could create entities, define relationships, and generate SQL scripts for my designs. This visual representation made it easy to conceptualize how different tables interacted, enhancing my understanding of relational database design. I spent hours experimenting with different models, iterating on my designs until they perfectly reflected my data needs.

The **Query Builder** was another feature that intrigued me. It allowed me to construct queries visually, dragging and dropping tables to create complex joins without having to remember intricate SQL syntax. This tool was invaluable for quickly building queries, especially as I ventured into more advanced SQL concepts like subqueries and aggregate functions. I appreciated how it streamlined the process, allowing me to focus on the logic of my queries rather than getting lost in syntax.

As I grew more comfortable with the software, I began to leverage the **Database Administration** tools. I was fascinated by the ability to manage user accounts, permissions, and even monitor server performance—all from within MySQL Workbench. It felt empowering to have such control over my database environment. I learned how to create new users, grant permissions, and ensure that my data remained secure. Each administrative task further solidified my understanding of how databases operate behind the scenes.

Backups and migrations were also essential aspects of database management, and MySQL Workbench provided tools to handle these tasks efficiently. I discovered the **Data Export** feature, which allowed me to create backups of my databases quickly. This functionality became a vital part of my workflow, ensuring that my data was safe and easily restorable in case of an unexpected failure. Similarly, the **Data Import** feature made it simple to migrate data from other sources, seamlessly integrating it into my MySQL databases.

One day, while working on a project, I realized I needed to visualize my data in a more dynamic way. This led me to explore the **Report** feature within MySQL Workbench. I could generate custom reports based on my queries, exporting them in various formats. This feature became invaluable for presenting insights to stakeholders, turning raw data into meaningful narratives.

As I continued to work with MySQL Workbench, I appreciated how it enhanced my productivity and confidence as a database developer. The combination of powerful features, intuitive design, and the ability to visualize my data made it an indispensable tool in my journey. Each new query I wrote, each database I managed, and each model I created felt like a step toward mastery.

Reflecting on my experience with MySQL Workbench, I realized that it was more than just a software application; it was a gateway to understanding the complexities of data management. The lessons I learned and the skills I developed while using Workbench would shape my approach to database design and query optimization for years to come. As I closed the application at the end of each day, I felt a sense of accomplishment, knowing that I was continuously growing as a developer, equipped with the tools to harness the power of MySQL effectively.

Basic Syntax

As my exploration of MySQL progressed, I quickly realized that understanding the basic syntax was fundamental to my journey into the realm of database management. The beauty of SQL lies in its simplicity and precision. It was like learning a new language, where each command held the power to manipulate data, create structures, and extract insights. This realization sparked a deeper curiosity within me to master the syntax that would enable me to communicate effectively with my databases.

I began by immersing myself in the four primary SQL operations, often referred to as CRUD: Create, Read, Update, and Delete. Each operation corresponds to a specific SQL statement that I needed to master, and I embraced the challenge with enthusiasm.

Creating Tables

The first step in my journey was to understand how to create tables. A table is the backbone of any database, acting as a structured format for storing data. The SQL command for creating a table is straightforward: CREATE TABLE. I eagerly crafted my first table, defining its structure with various columns and data types.

```
CREATE TABLE employees (
    id INT AUTO_INCREMENT PRIMARY KEY,
    name VARCHAR(100) NOT NULL,
    position VARCHAR(50),
    hire_date DATE,
    salary DECIMAL(10, 2)
);
```

In this example, I defined an employees table with columns for employee ID, name, position, hire date, and salary. The use of AUTO_INCREMENT for the ID column was particularly fascinating, as it allowed MySQL to automatically generate unique IDs for each new record. I felt a sense of accomplishment as I executed this command, watching my first table take shape.

Inserting Data

With my table created, the next logical step was to insert data into it. The INSERT INTO statement would become one of my best friends in SQL. I practiced adding records to my table, experimenting with different data types and formats. Each successful insertion reinforced my understanding of how data flows into a database.

INSERT INTO employees (name, position, hire_date, salary)

VALUES ('Alice Johnson', 'Software Engineer', '2024-01-15', 75000.00), ('Bob Smith', 'Project Manager', '2024-02-20', 85000.00);

Seeing my data populate the table was exhilarating. I could now visualize how the database would function, with each record representing an employee and their respective details. It was a tangible representation of the abstract concepts I had been learning.

Querying Data

As I became more comfortable with inserting data, I was eager to explore how to retrieve it. The SELECT statement became my gateway to understanding how to query the database. I learned to extract specific information by using SELECT alongside various clauses such as WHERE, ORDER BY, and LIMIT.

*SELECT * FROM employees WHERE position = 'Software Engineer' ORDER BY hire_date DESC;*

This query allowed me to filter and sort the data, showcasing my growing ability to manipulate information. I could see how powerful the SELECT statement was, enabling me to answer specific questions about my data set with ease. Each successful query felt like uncovering a hidden insight, reinforcing my desire to dig deeper into the data.

Updating Data

With a solid grasp of querying, I turned my attention to updating existing records using the UPDATE statement. I found it fascinating that I could modify specific entries in my database while leaving others untouched. This ability to refine data was crucial for maintaining accuracy and relevance within my tables.

UPDATE employees SET salary = 80000.00 WHERE name = 'Alice Johnson';

Executing this command felt empowering; I was actively managing the data to reflect real-world changes. Each update reinforced the idea that data is not static but rather a living entity that evolves over time.

Deleting Data

As I ventured further, I also had to confront the concept of data deletion. The DELETE statement allowed me to remove records that were no longer relevant or needed. While it was sometimes bittersweet to delete data, I understood that maintaining a clean and organized database was essential for effective management.

DELETE FROM employees WHERE name = 'Bob Smith';

Executing this command brought a mix of relief and responsibility. I realized that with great power comes great responsibility. Deleting data required careful consideration, as it could not be undone without a backup.

Combining Statements

As I continued to practice these basic operations, I began to experiment with combining statements and using joins to retrieve data from multiple tables. Understanding the nuances of how different tables could interact opened up a whole new world of possibilities. I learned about inner joins, outer joins, and self-joins, each allowing me to extract richer insights from my databases.

SELECT employees.name, departments.name FROM employees JOIN departments ON employees.department_id = departments.id;

The ability to merge data from different tables created a more comprehensive picture of my database landscape. I felt a sense of achievement as I crafted complex queries, each one revealing deeper connections and insights within my data.

Reflecting on my journey through the basic syntax of MySQL, I recognized how each operation contributed to my growing expertise. The simplicity of SQL syntax belied its power, and I felt increasingly confident in my ability to communicate with my databases. The foundational skills I acquired during this phase would serve as building blocks for more advanced concepts and techniques in the future.

Each command I executed became a stepping stone, guiding me toward mastery of MySQL. I realized that this was just the beginning—my journey into the world of databases had only just begun, and I was excited to continue exploring the endless possibilities that MySQL had to offer. As I wrote and executed queries, I felt a newfound sense of freedom and creativity, ready to tackle the challenges ahead.

Inserting Data

As I delved deeper into the world of MySQL, the next crucial topic on my journey was understanding how to insert data into my tables. This process, though seemingly straightforward, was fundamental to populating my database and enabling meaningful interactions with the data I would store. I felt a sense of anticipation as I prepared to learn the intricacies of the INSERT statement, knowing that this would be my gateway to creating a vibrant, functional database.

The INSERT Statement

The INSERT statement is the primary means by which I would add new records to my tables. The basic syntax of the INSERT INTO statement is simple and intuitive:

INSERT INTO table_name (column1, column2, column3, ...)
VALUES (value1, value2, value3, ...);

This structure clearly delineates where the new data would be placed within the specified columns of my chosen table. The process became clearer as I practiced writing these commands. I began with my employees table, excited to see how I could fill it with meaningful data.

Inserting Single Records

To get started, I executed my first INSERT command, adding a single record to the employees table:

INSERT INTO employees (name, position, hire_date, salary) VALUES ('John Doe', 'Database Administrator', '2024-03-01', 90000.00);

Executing this command filled me with satisfaction as I saw how easily I could add an employee's information to my database. The record now existed within the employees table, and I felt a sense of accomplishment at having successfully populated my first entry.

Inserting Multiple Records

As I grew more confident, I began to explore the ability to insert multiple records simultaneously. This feature was particularly advantageous when I had several entries to add at once, saving me from the repetitive task of executing multiple INSERT statements. I experimented with this feature, inserting several employees in one go:

INSERT INTO employees (name, position, hire_date, salary)

VALUES ('Alice Johnson', 'Software Engineer', '2024-01-15', 75000.00), ('Bob Smith', 'Project Manager', '2024-02-20', 85000.00), ('Charlie Brown', 'Data Analyst', '2024-03-10', 70000.00);

With a single execution, I populated my table with three new entries, marveling at the efficiency of the command. Each record added depth to my database, and I could visualize a growing roster of employees, each with their own unique details.

Using Default Values

Another essential aspect of inserting data was understanding how to use default values. When creating a table, I had the option to specify default values for certain columns, ensuring that if I didn't provide data during an insertion, MySQL would automatically fill those fields with predefined values. This became particularly useful for columns like hire_date, where I wanted to record the current date if no specific date was provided.

For example, if I defined my hire_date column with a default value of the current date, I could insert a new employee without explicitly specifying the hire date:

INSERT INTO employees (name, position, salary)
VALUES ('David Wilson', 'Intern', 40000.00);

In this instance, the hire_date would automatically populate with the current date, showcasing how default values could streamline my data insertion process.

Handling NULL Values

I also learned to manage NULL values, which represent the absence of a value. It was crucial to understand when to insert NULL and how to handle columns that allowed it. If a particular piece of information was unknown or not applicable, I could explicitly insert NULL:

INSERT INTO employees (name, position, hire_date, salary) VALUES ('Eva Green', NULL, '2024-04-01', 50000.00);

In this command, I chose to leave the position field as NULL, signifying that the information was not yet determined. This flexibility allowed my database to accurately reflect real-world scenarios where data may not always be available.

The Importance of Data Types

Understanding data types became paramount as I inserted records. Each column in my table had a specified data type, dictating what kind of data could be stored. For example, I learned that the salary column should be a DECIMAL type to handle monetary values accurately, while hire_date needed to be of type DATE to store date information correctly.

I made sure to adhere to these data types during insertion, as attempting to insert incompatible data would result in an error. For instance, trying to insert a string value into an integer column would prompt MySQL to reject the operation, reinforcing the importance of matching data types correctly.

Error Handling During Insertion

As I practiced inserting data, I encountered the inevitable errors that come with learning. One of the most common errors involved attempting to insert a record without satisfying all constraints defined in the table. For instance, if I attempted to insert a record without providing a value for a column defined as NOT NULL, MySQL would return an error.

To handle these situations gracefully, I learned to read error messages carefully, understanding what went wrong and how to fix it. This iterative process became an essential part of my learning, allowing me to refine my skills and ensure that my data was inserted correctly.

Inserting data into MySQL tables became an exhilarating part of my journey into database management. Each successful insertion brought my database to life, allowing me to manipulate and manage data in meaningful ways. The simplicity of the INSERT statement belied its power, enabling me to build a robust repository of information that could be queried and analyzed.

As I continued to practice and explore, I developed a deeper understanding of how to effectively manage data within MySQL. I realized that mastering the art of data insertion was not merely about adding records; it was about creating a dynamic environment where information could be transformed into insights. With each new record, I felt more connected to my database, excited about the possibilities that lay ahead in my exploration of MySQL.

Query Data

As I progressed in my journey through MySQL, the next logical step was to delve into querying data. This aspect of database management was nothing short of exhilarating. Querying allowed me to extract meaningful insights from the vast sea of information I had started to build in my database. I understood that mastering the art of querying was crucial for transforming raw data into actionable intelligence.

The SELECT Statement

At the heart of querying data in MySQL lies the SELECT statement. This powerful command enables me to retrieve data from one or more tables, providing the foundation for data analysis. The basic syntax of the SELECT statement is simple yet flexible:

SELECT column1, column2, ...
FROM table_name;

This structure gave me the ability to specify which columns I wanted to see, along with the source table from which the data would be extracted. I began experimenting with simple queries, extracting data from my employees table to see the fruits of my earlier efforts.

Retrieving All Columns

One of the first things I learned was how to retrieve all columns from a table. This was a straightforward yet powerful technique, particularly when I wanted a comprehensive view of all the records in a table. To accomplish this, I used the asterisk (*) wildcard:

SELECT * FROM employees;

Executing this command filled my screen with a complete list of employees, showcasing all the information stored in my table. Seeing the data laid out in front of me was incredibly rewarding, as it affirmed that my previous data insertions were successful.

Filtering Results with WHERE

As I grew more comfortable with retrieving data, I quickly realized the importance of filtering results to hone in on specific information. The WHERE clause became my go-to tool for this purpose, allowing me to set conditions that the retrieved records had to meet.

For instance, if I wanted to find all employees in a particular position, I crafted a query like this:

SELECT * FROM employees WHERE position = 'Software Engineer';

This query narrowed my focus, returning only those records that matched my specified criteria. It was like having a powerful magnifying glass that allowed me to sift through vast amounts of data and extract precisely what I was looking for.

Sorting Results with ORDER BY

In addition to filtering, I discovered the value of sorting my query results for better readability and analysis. The ORDER BY clause enabled me to arrange the retrieved data in ascending or descending order based on one or more columns.

For example, if I wanted to see my employees sorted by their hire date, I could execute:

*SELECT * FROM employees ORDER BY hire_date ASC;*

The results were now neatly organized, allowing me to visualize the sequence in which employees joined the company. Sorting data added an extra layer of clarity to my analysis, making it easier to identify trends or patterns.

Limiting Results with LIMIT

As I continued to explore, I learned about the LIMIT clause, which proved invaluable for managing large data sets. By specifying a limit, I could control how many records to return, making it easier to digest and analyze results.

For instance, if I wanted to see only the first five employees in my table, I could write:

SELECT * FROM employees LIMIT 5;

This command kept my output concise, allowing me to focus on a manageable subset of data. It was especially useful when I needed to preview results or when working with extensive tables.

Combining Filters and Sorting

The real power of querying emerged when I began to combine filters, sorting, and limits into more complex queries. I realized I could create sophisticated queries that provided rich insights by layering conditions.

For example, I wanted to find the top three highest-paid employees in the Software Engineer position, sorted by salary. I crafted the following query:

SELECT *
FROM employees
WHERE position = 'Software Engineer'
ORDER BY salary DESC
LIMIT 3;

Executing this command provided me with a precise snapshot of my top earners, showcasing the ability to synthesize various query components into a single operation. It was an empowering realization of the flexibility that SQL offered.

Using Aggregate Functions

As I advanced in my querying journey, I encountered aggregate functions, which allowed me to perform calculations on sets of data. Functions like COUNT(), SUM(), AVG(), MIN(), and MAX() became invaluable tools for analyzing my data.

For example, I used the COUNT() function to determine the total number of employees:

SELECT COUNT(*) FROM employees;

This command returned a single value representing the total number of records in my table. I also learned to use SUM() to calculate the total salary expenditure for all employees:

SELECT SUM(salary) FROM employees;

These aggregate functions enriched my analytical capabilities, enabling me to derive deeper insights from my data set.

Grouping Data with GROUP BY

To further enhance my analytical prowess, I discovered the GROUP BY clause, which allowed me to organize my query results based on specific columns. This was particularly useful when I wanted to analyze data across different categories.

For instance, if I wanted to know the average salary of employees by position, I crafted the following query:

SELECT position, AVG(salary) FROM employees
GROUP BY position;

This command grouped my results by position, providing the average salary for each role within the company. The ability to aggregate and group data in this way opened new avenues for understanding trends and patterns within my employee data.

Joining Tables

As I explored further, I learned about the concept of joining tables, which allowed me to retrieve data from multiple related tables in a single query. This capability was crucial for synthesizing information across different aspects of my database.

For instance, if I had a departments table that listed department details, I could join it with my employees table to see which employees belonged to which departments:

SELECT employees.name, departments.name
FROM employees
JOIN departments ON employees.department_id = departments.id;

This join operation enabled me to create a more comprehensive view of my data, showcasing relationships between different entities within my database.

Querying data in MySQL became a cornerstone of my database management journey. Each SELECT statement I crafted brought me closer to unlocking the potential hidden within my data. The ability to filter, sort, limit, and aggregate results transformed the way I interacted with my database, allowing me to derive meaningful insights and make informed decisions.

As I practiced querying, I felt increasingly confident in my ability to extract valuable information from my data set. I realized that mastering the art of querying was not just about retrieving records but about understanding the stories that data could tell. With each new query, I felt empowered to uncover deeper truths within my database, excited about the possibilities that lay ahead as I continued to explore the world of MySQL.

Filtering Results

As I continued to navigate the intricities of MySQL, one of the most powerful capabilities I discovered was filtering results. The ability to retrieve only the data that meets specific criteria was not just a convenience; it was an essential skill that transformed my database interactions into targeted and efficient explorations of information. Filtering allowed me to sift through vast amounts of data, honing in on exactly what I needed to answer pressing questions or uncover valuable insights.

The WHERE Clause

At the core of filtering results is the WHERE clause. This fundamental aspect of SQL enables me to specify conditions that the retrieved records must satisfy. By using the WHERE clause, I could define criteria based on the values in specific columns, effectively narrowing down my result set to only those rows that were relevant to my query.

For instance, if I wanted to extract all employees who worked in the 'Marketing' department, I crafted a query like this:

*SELECT * FROM employees WHERE department = 'Marketing';*

This simple yet effective statement returned a focused view of my data, showcasing only the employees in the specified department. As I executed the command, the joy of seeing filtered results reinforced my understanding of the power of the WHERE clause.

Comparison Operators

The ability to use comparison operators expanded my filtering capabilities significantly. Operators such as =, !=, >, <, >=, and <= allowed me to create precise conditions based on numeric and string comparisons. This versatility meant I could filter results based on any criterion that was essential for my analysis.

For example, if I wanted to find employees whose salary exceeded $70,000, I could write:

*SELECT * FROM employees WHERE salary > 70000;*

This command brought forth only those employees earning more than the specified threshold, enabling me to identify higher earners within my organization.

Logical Operators

As I ventured deeper into filtering, I learned about logical operators: AND, OR, and NOT. These operators provided a way to combine multiple conditions in a single query, allowing me to filter results with greater complexity and nuance.

For example, if I wanted to find employees in the 'Sales' department who earned more than $60,000, I could use the AND operator:

SELECT * FROM employees WHERE department = 'Sales' AND salary > 60000;

In contrast, if I wanted to find employees in either the 'Marketing' or 'Sales' departments, I could leverage the OR operator:

SELECT * FROM employees WHERE department = 'Marketing' OR department = 'Sales';

The NOT operator also became useful in my quest for filtering results. For instance, if I wanted to find all employees who did not work in the 'HR' department, I could use:

SELECT * FROM employees WHERE department != 'HR';

Combining these logical operators enriched my querying abilities, allowing me to tailor my results precisely to my needs.

Using LIKE for Pattern Matching

The LIKE operator opened up a world of possibilities for filtering text-based data. This operator allowed me to perform pattern matching on string columns, making it particularly useful when I didn't know the exact value I was searching for or when I wanted to find similar entries.

For instance, if I wanted to find all employees whose names began with the letter 'J', I could construct a query like this:

*SELECT * FROM employees WHERE name LIKE 'J%';*

The % wildcard character indicated that any sequence of characters could follow 'J', returning a list of all employees whose names fit that pattern. Similarly, I could use LIKE with the _ wildcard to match a single character.

For example, to find employees whose names had 'o' as the second character, I could write:

*SELECT * FROM employees WHERE name LIKE '_o%';*

These pattern-matching capabilities made my queries far more dynamic and flexible, enabling me to explore my data in innovative ways.

Filtering with IN and BETWEEN

The IN operator provided a powerful mechanism for filtering results based on a list of values. Instead of using multiple OR conditions, I could succinctly specify multiple values in a single clause. For example, if I wanted to find employees in the 'HR', 'Sales', or 'IT' departments, I could write:

SELECT * FROM employees WHERE department IN ('HR', 'Sales', 'IT');

This concise syntax streamlined my queries, enhancing both readability and efficiency.

Similarly, the BETWEEN operator allowed me to filter results based on a range of values. If I wanted to find employees whose hire dates fell between January 1, 2020, and December 31, 2022, I could construct the following query:

SELECT * FROM employees WHERE hire_date BETWEEN '2020-01-01' AND '2022-12-31';

This functionality empowered me to filter results based on temporal data, making it easier to analyze trends over specific periods.

NULL Values

As I became more proficient in filtering, I also learned to handle NULL values in my queries. NULL values represented the absence of data and required special consideration in filtering. To filter for records with NULL values in a specific column, I used the IS NULL condition. Conversely, to find records where a column did not contain NULL values, I used IS NOT NULL.

For example, to find employees without a specified hire date, I could write:

SELECT * FROM employees WHERE hire_date IS NULL;

Understanding how to filter NULL values enhanced my ability to work with incomplete data sets, ensuring that I could derive meaningful insights even when faced with gaps in the information.

Combining Filters for Complex Queries

As my skills advanced, I began combining various filtering techniques to create complex queries that addressed specific business questions. I could now construct queries that not only filtered results based on multiple criteria but also incorporated different operators and functions.

For example, if I wanted to find employees in the 'Engineering' department who had been hired after 2019 and earned more than $80,000, I could write:

*SELECT * FROM employees*

WHERE department = 'Engineering'

AND hire_date > '2019-01-01'

AND salary > 80000;

This ability to construct sophisticated queries meant that I could uncover nuanced insights from my data, answering questions that required detailed analysis.

Filtering results in MySQL was a transformative aspect of my database journey. The WHERE clause, combined with comparison operators, logical operators, and specialized functions like LIKE, IN, and BETWEEN, allowed me to hone in on specific data points with precision.

As I crafted more complex queries, I realized that filtering was not just about narrowing down results; it was about storytelling with data. Each filtered query provided a glimpse into the underlying narratives within my database, revealing patterns, trends, and insights that were crucial for informed decision-making.

With every new filtering technique I mastered, I felt a growing sense of confidence in my ability to interact with my data effectively. The skills I developed in filtering results laid the foundation for deeper analytical work, enabling me to draw meaningful conclusions and ultimately enriching my overall experience with MySQL.

Order Results

As I delved deeper into MySQL, I discovered that retrieving data was only part of the equation. Once I had filtered the results, the next step was to present that data in a way that was easy to analyze and understand. This is where the ORDER BY clause came into play. By ordering results, I could not only enhance the readability of my queries but also uncover trends and insights that might not have been immediately apparent in a jumbled list.

The ORDER BY Clause

The ORDER BY clause allowed me to sort the results of my queries based on one or more columns. This capability was essential for organizing data in a manner that made sense for my analysis. Whether I wanted to arrange employees by their hire dates, salaries, or departments, the ORDER BY clause provided a straightforward syntax to achieve this.

For example, if I wanted to retrieve all employees and sort them by their last names in ascending order, I would write:

SELECT * FROM employees ORDER BY last_name ASC;

In this query, the ASC keyword specified that the results should be sorted in ascending order (from A to Z). If I wanted to reverse this order and see the employees listed from Z to A, I could simply change ASC to DESC:

SELECT * FROM employees ORDER BY last_name DESC;

This ability to sort data according to my preferences dramatically improved my ability to analyze the information presented.

Sorting by Multiple Columns

As I continued to explore the ORDER BY clause, I learned that I could also sort results by multiple columns simultaneously. This functionality was particularly useful when I wanted to refine my sorting criteria further. For instance, if I wanted to sort employees first by department and then by salary within each department, I could construct a query like this:

SELECT * FROM employees ORDER BY department ASC, salary DESC;

In this case, the results would first be grouped by department in ascending order, and within each department, employees would be sorted by salary in descending order. This multi-level sorting not only organized my data more effectively but also allowed me to compare different subsets within the overall dataset.

Sorting with NULL Values

One aspect of sorting that I found particularly intriguing was how NULL values were handled. In MySQL, NULL values were sorted in a specific order depending on whether I used ASC or DESC. When sorting in ascending order, NULL values would appear first, while in descending order, they would appear last. This behavior was crucial to keep in mind, especially when I needed to analyze data that contained missing entries.

For example, if I executed the following query:

SELECT * FROM employees ORDER BY salary ASC;

Any employees with NULL values in the salary column would appear at the top of the results, potentially skewing my analysis if I wasn't aware of this sorting behavior. To mitigate this, I often used techniques to handle NULL values appropriately, such as replacing them with default values or filtering them out entirely before sorting.

Case Sensitivity in Sorting

Another nuanced aspect of sorting results was case sensitivity. By default, MySQL treated string comparisons as case-insensitive, which meant that uppercase and lowercase letters were considered equal when sorting. However, depending on the collation settings of the column, this behavior could change.

For instance, if I wanted to sort a list of employee names and ensure that names beginning with uppercase letters appeared before those with lowercase letters, I could specify a binary collation for the sorting operation:

*SELECT * FROM employees ORDER BY BINARY first_name;*

This query would enforce case sensitivity, allowing me to present my results in a way that highlighted the differences between uppercase and lowercase entries. Understanding this behavior allowed me to maintain control over how my data was presented, ensuring clarity in my analysis.

Sorting with Aliases

As I became more comfortable with SQL, I also discovered that I could enhance the clarity of my results by using aliases in my queries. Aliases provided a way to give temporary names to columns, which could be particularly useful when sorting results based on calculated fields or when using complex expressions.

For example, if I wanted to order employees based on a calculated bonus that I derived from their salary, I could create an alias for that calculation:

SELECT first_name, last_name, salary, (salary * 0.10) AS bonus

FROM employees

ORDER BY bonus DESC;

In this query, I calculated a 10% bonus based on the salary and sorted the results by the calculated bonus in descending order. Using aliases not only made my queries easier to read but also added a layer of flexibility that enhanced my ability to sort results based on various conditions.

The ability to order results in MySQL was a significant advancement in my data manipulation journey. The ORDER BY clause empowered me to present my queries in a structured and logical manner, enhancing the clarity and usability of the information retrieved.

By learning to sort results by single or multiple columns, handle NULL values, and utilize case sensitivity, I was able to derive meaningful insights from my data with greater efficiency. Additionally, the use of aliases added a level of sophistication to my queries, enabling me to present calculated fields with ease.

As I continued to refine my skills in ordering results, I recognized that this capability was not just about arranging data; it was about telling a story with my information.

Each ordered query provided a clear narrative, guiding me through the insights hidden within my database and empowering me to make informed decisions based on the data at hand. This journey into ordering results not only solidified my understanding of SQL but also enriched my overall experience as I explored the world of MySQL.

Limit Results

As I continued my journey with MySQL, I quickly realized that while retrieving data is essential, it's equally important to manage the volume of information returned by queries. In many scenarios, especially when dealing with large datasets, the need to limit the number of results became apparent. This is where the LIMIT clause became an invaluable tool in my SQL toolkit.

The LIMIT Clause

The LIMIT clause allows you to specify the maximum number of records to return from a query. This feature is particularly useful when you only need a subset of the total results, whether for performance reasons, user interface constraints, or simply to focus on a specific segment of data. For example, if I wanted to fetch just the first five employees from a list, I would write:

SELECT * FROM employees LIMIT 5;

In this query, MySQL would return only the first five records from the employees table. This capability not only improved the performance of my queries but also helped me manage the display of information in my applications.

Offset with LIMIT

As I explored the LIMIT clause further, I discovered the ability to use an offset alongside it, providing even greater control over which records to retrieve. The offset allows you to skip a specified number of rows before beginning to return the results. This functionality is especially beneficial for pagination, where I needed to display results across multiple pages.

For instance, if I wanted to retrieve the second set of five employees (i.e., records 6 to 10), I could modify my query as follows:

*SELECT * FROM employees LIMIT 5 OFFSET 5;*

Alternatively, I could use a more concise syntax by combining the two values in a single LIMIT statement:

SELECT * FROM employees LIMIT 5, 5;

Both of these queries would yield the same results, retrieving the sixth through tenth employees. This capability to paginate results opened up a world of possibilities for presenting data in my applications, allowing users to navigate through large datasets smoothly.

Use Cases for Limiting Results

Throughout my exploration, I encountered numerous scenarios where limiting results proved beneficial. One common use case was when I needed to display a leaderboard or top-performing entries. For instance, if I wanted to show the top five employees with the highest salaries, I could combine the ORDER BY clause with LIMIT:

*SELECT * FROM employees ORDER BY salary DESC LIMIT 5;*

This query would return the five employees with the highest salaries, providing a concise view of top performers. The ability to limit results made it easy to generate reports and insights based on specific criteria, streamlining the decision-making process.

Performance Considerations

While the LIMIT clause greatly enhanced my ability to manage query results, I also became aware of performance considerations when using it. When working with large tables, applying LIMIT without an appropriate ORDER BY clause could yield unpredictable results. Without a defined order, the rows returned could vary between executions, making it challenging to rely on the consistency of the data presented.

For example, if I executed a query like this:

*SELECT * FROM employees LIMIT 5;*

The five records returned could change with each execution if no ordering was applied. To ensure consistent results, I made it a practice to always pair LIMIT with an ORDER BY clause, thus solidifying the reliability of my queries.

Mastering the LIMIT clause was a pivotal moment in my MySQL journey. It not only allowed me to control the volume of data returned by my queries but also opened up new avenues for data presentation, particularly in terms of pagination and focused reporting.

By learning to combine LIMIT with ORDER BY and understanding the importance of consistent ordering, I could effectively navigate large datasets and extract meaningful insights without overwhelming myself or the users of my applications.

This newfound ability to limit results transformed how I approached data retrieval, empowering me to present information in a more organized, user-friendly manner. As I continued to work with MySQL, I embraced the principle that sometimes, less is indeed more, and the effective use of the LIMIT clause exemplified this perfectly.

Updating Data

As I progressed further in my journey with MySQL, I soon encountered the need to modify existing records in my database. Whether it was correcting a typographical error, adjusting a value based on new information, or updating the status of an order, the ability to update data efficiently was essential. This is where the UPDATE statement became a fundamental part of my SQL toolkit.

The UPDATE Statement

The UPDATE statement allows you to modify existing records in a table. Its syntax is straightforward, yet powerful, enabling me to specify which table to update, what values to change, and under what conditions. The basic syntax for an UPDATE statement is as follows:

UPDATE table_name

SET column1 = value1, column2 = value2

WHERE condition;

In this statement, table_name refers to the table containing the records I want to update, column1 and column2 are the specific columns whose values I want to change, and the WHERE clause identifies which records should be modified.

Executing a Basic Update

One of my first practical applications of the UPDATE statement was to correct an employee's job title. If an employee named John Doe had been mistakenly entered with the job title "Software Engineer" instead of "Senior Software Engineer," I would use the following query:

UPDATE employees

SET job_title = 'Senior Software Engineer'

WHERE first_name = 'John' AND last_name = 'Doe';

This query effectively updated John Doe's job title by targeting only the specific record that met the conditions specified in the WHERE clause. The precision of the WHERE clause was crucial, as it ensured that only the intended record was modified, preventing any unintended updates to other employees.

Updating Multiple Records

As I became more comfortable with the UPDATE statement, I learned that it was also possible to update multiple records simultaneously. If I needed to adjust the salary of all employees in a particular department due to a company-wide raise, I could execute a query like this:

UPDATE employees

SET salary = salary * 1.10

WHERE department = 'Sales';

In this example, all employees in the Sales department received a 10% salary increase. This powerful capability allowed me to implement changes across multiple records with a single command, significantly improving my efficiency when managing the data.

The Importance of the WHERE Clause

Throughout my experiences, I quickly understood that the WHERE clause was paramount when using the UPDATE statement. Omitting the WHERE clause would result in updating every record in the table, which could lead to catastrophic data loss or corruption. For instance, executing the following query would change the job title of every employee to "Updated Title":

UPDATE employees

SET job_title = 'Updated Title';

To avoid such pitfalls, I made it a habit to double-check my queries, especially when executing updates. I often performed a SELECT query with the same WHERE conditions before executing an update, allowing me to review the records that would be affected.

Transactions and Data Integrity

As I delved deeper into MySQL, I discovered the importance of transactions, especially when performing updates. A transaction allows you to group a series of SQL operations into a single unit of work. If any part of the transaction fails, you can roll back the entire transaction to maintain data integrity.

To implement a transaction while updating data, I would use the following commands:

START TRANSACTION;

UPDATE employees

SET salary = salary * 1.10

WHERE department = 'Sales';

-- Assuming a check for errors occurs here

COMMIT;

By wrapping my update operations in a transaction, I could ensure that my database remained consistent, even in the event of an error or unexpected issue during the update process.

The ability to update data in MySQL was a critical skill that significantly enhanced my database management capabilities. With the UPDATE statement, I could efficiently correct errors, implement changes, and manage records to reflect the most current information.

By mastering the syntax and best practices associated with updates, including the importance of the WHERE clause and the use of transactions, I could navigate the complexities of data modification with confidence. This skill not only empowered me to keep my database accurate and up-to-date but also reinforced the principle of data integrity, which became a cornerstone of my approach to database management.

As I continued my journey with MySQL, I embraced the idea that maintaining accurate and timely data was essential to deriving meaningful insights and making informed decisions, and the ability to update records effectively was a key component of that mission.

Deleting Data

As I progressed further in my MySQL journey, I soon confronted the reality that managing data wasn't just about inserting, updating, and retrieving—it also involved the crucial task of deleting unnecessary or obsolete records. Whether it was removing a temporary entry, deleting outdated information, or cleaning up after an error, the DELETE statement became an indispensable tool in my SQL arsenal.

The DELETE Statement

The DELETE statement is designed to remove existing records from a table. Its syntax is relatively simple, yet powerful, allowing me to specify which table to target and under what conditions. The basic structure of the DELETE statement is as follows:

DELETE FROM table_name

WHERE condition;

In this statement, table_name refers to the table from which I want to delete records, and the WHERE clause specifies the criteria that determine which records should be removed. Just like with the UPDATE statement, the WHERE clause plays a vital role in ensuring that only the intended records are deleted.

Executing a Basic Delete

One of my initial experiences with the DELETE statement involved removing a specific employee record from the database. If I needed to delete an employee named John Doe due to a data entry error, I would execute the following query:

DELETE FROM employees

WHERE first_name = 'John' AND last_name = 'Doe';

This query effectively removed the record of John Doe from the employees table, ensuring that my database remained accurate and up-to-date. The precision of the WHERE clause was crucial here, as it safeguarded against the accidental deletion of other employee records.

Deleting Multiple Records

As I became more adept at using the DELETE statement, I discovered that it could also be employed to delete multiple records at once. For instance, if I wanted to remove all employees in a specific department that had been dissolved, I could execute a query like this:

DELETE FROM employees

WHERE department = 'Sales';

In this scenario, all records associated with the Sales department would be deleted in one swift operation. This capability was incredibly useful when managing large datasets, allowing me to perform bulk deletions efficiently.

The Importance of the WHERE Clause

Throughout my journey, I learned that the WHERE clause was paramount when using the DELETE statement. Omitting this clause could lead to the catastrophic removal of every record in the table, which would not only be destructive but could also result in significant data loss.

For example, executing the following query would delete all employees from the table:

DELETE FROM employees;

To prevent such disasters, I made it a practice to double-check my queries, especially before executing deletes. I often performed a SELECT query with the same WHERE conditions to verify the records that would be affected by the delete operation.

Transactions and Data Integrity

As I advanced in my understanding of MySQL, I became increasingly aware of the importance of transactions, particularly when performing delete operations. A transaction allows me to group a series of SQL operations into a single unit of work, ensuring that if any part of the transaction fails, I can roll back the entire operation to maintain data integrity.

To implement a transaction while deleting data, I would use the following commands:

START TRANSACTION;

DELETE FROM employees

WHERE department = 'Sales';

-- Assuming a check for errors occurs here

COMMIT;

By wrapping my delete operations in a transaction, I could ensure that my database remained consistent, even in the event of an error during the delete process. This approach provided me with greater control and peace of mind when managing my data.

The ability to delete data in MySQL was a vital skill that allowed me to maintain the integrity and accuracy of my database. With the DELETE statement, I could efficiently remove unnecessary records and keep my datasets clean and relevant.

By mastering the syntax and best practices associated with deletions, including the critical importance of the WHERE clause and the use of transactions, I could navigate the complexities of data management with confidence. This skill not only empowered me to maintain an accurate database but also reinforced the principle of data integrity, which became a cornerstone of my approach to database management.

As I continued my journey with MySQL, I embraced the idea that effective data management was not just about adding and modifying records but also about knowing when to let go of unnecessary data. The DELETE statement exemplified this principle, reminding me that maintaining a clean and organized database was essential for deriving meaningful insights and making informed decisions.

Using Aliases

As I delved deeper into the intricacies of MySQL, I discovered the power of aliases—a feature that would prove invaluable in enhancing the readability and clarity of my SQL queries. Aliases allow me to create temporary names for tables or columns, making my queries more understandable, especially when dealing with complex joins, aggregations, or when I needed to distinguish between similar columns in my result set.

What Are Aliases?

In SQL, an alias is a temporary name given to a table or a column for the duration of a query. This feature is particularly useful when the original names are lengthy, unwieldy, or when I wanted to simplify my output for better comprehension. Aliases are defined using the AS keyword, although this keyword is optional in MySQL.

Creating Column Aliases

One of my earliest applications of aliases involved creating more meaningful or simpler names for the columns in my result set. For instance, suppose I had a table called employees, which included columns like first_name, last_name, and hire_date. When retrieving data from this table, I could enhance the readability of my output by using aliases:

SELECT first_name AS 'First Name',

    last_name AS 'Last Name',

    hire_date AS 'Date of Hire'

FROM employees;

In this query, I replaced the original column names with more descriptive aliases, which made the output easier to read and understand, especially for anyone unfamiliar with the database schema. The aliases provided a clearer context, transforming the raw data into a more user-friendly format.

Creating Table Aliases

Aliases are equally beneficial when working with multiple tables, especially during join operations. For example, if I wanted to retrieve data from both the employees table and a departments table, I could use aliases to simplify my queries and avoid ambiguity:

SELECT e.first_name AS 'Employee First Name',

    e.last_name AS 'Employee Last Name',

    d.department_name AS 'Department'

FROM employees AS e

JOIN departments AS d ON e.department_id = d.id;

In this example, I assigned the alias e to the employees table and d to the departments table. This shorthand made my query cleaner and less cluttered, making it easier to read and understand. Using table aliases is particularly useful in more complex queries where multiple tables are joined, as it reduces the need to repeatedly write out long table names.

Using Aliases in Aggregate Functions

As I explored aggregate functions like SUM(), AVG(), and COUNT(), I realized that aliases could also enhance the clarity of my output when performing calculations. For instance, if I wanted to calculate the total salaries of employees in each department, I could use an alias for the aggregated result:

SELECT d.department_name AS 'Department',

   SUM(e.salary) AS 'Total Salary'

FROM employees AS e

JOIN departments AS d ON e.department_id = d.id

GROUP BY d.department_name;

Here, I used the alias Total Salary to label the aggregated result of the SUM() function. This not only made the output more intuitive but also provided a clear understanding of what the calculated value represented.

Benefits of Using Aliases

Throughout my journey with MySQL, I learned that using aliases offered several benefits:

Improved Readability: Aliases make SQL queries more concise and easier to read, especially for those who may not be familiar with the underlying database structure.

Clearer Output: By providing meaningful names to columns and tables, aliases enhance the clarity of the output, making it easier to interpret the results.

Simplified Syntax: In complex queries involving multiple tables, aliases reduce the amount of typing required and minimize the potential for errors.

Contextual Clarity: Aliases can help clarify the context of data, particularly when dealing with similar column names across different tables.

The use of aliases in MySQL significantly enriched my SQL queries and the overall readability of my database interactions. By adopting this practice, I was able to create more understandable and intuitive queries, particularly when dealing with complex data structures.

Mastering aliases not only empowered me to write cleaner SQL code but also reinforced the principle that effective communication of data is as vital as the data itself. As I continued my journey with MySQL, I recognized that the clarity of my output could lead to more meaningful insights and better decision-making, making aliases an essential tool in my SQL toolkit.

Embracing the practice of using aliases transformed my approach to writing queries, allowing me to craft statements that were not only functional but also elegant and easy to understand. In the world of databases, where clarity is key, aliases proved to be a simple yet powerful ally in my quest for effective data management.

JOIN TABLES

Alright, now that you've learned how to create, select, and delete databases, it's time to dive into something a bit more advanced: **joining tables**.

WHAT IS A JOIN?

Think of it this way: imagine you have two tables, one with a list of **customers** and another with **orders**. If you want to see which customer placed which order, you need to connect these tables somehow. That's where **JOINs** come in!

A **JOIN** is a way to combine rows from two or more tables based on a related column between them. It allows you to see data from both tables in a single result set.

TYPES OF JOINS

MySQL supports several types of joins, but the most common ones are:

1. **INNER JOIN**: Returns only the rows that have matching values in both tables.
2. **LEFT JOIN (or LEFT OUTER JOIN)**: Returns all rows from the left table and the matching rows from the right table. If there's no match, the result is NULL on the right side.
3. **RIGHT JOIN (or RIGHT OUTER JOIN)**: Opposite of LEFT JOIN. It returns all rows from the right table and the matching rows from the left.
4. **FULL JOIN (or FULL OUTER JOIN)**: Returns all rows when there is a match in either the left or the right table. If there's no match, the result is NULL on either

side. *(Note: MySQL doesn't natively support FULL JOIN, but you can achieve it using UNION.)*

INNER JOIN EXAMPLE

Let's start with the most common type: **INNER JOIN**.

Suppose we have two tables:

- customers
- orders

The customers table looks like this:

customer_id	customer_name
1	Alice
2	Bob
3	Charlie

And the orders table looks like this:

order_id	customer_id	order_date
101	1	2024-09-20
102	2	2024-09-21
103	1	2024-09-22

Now, if you want to see which customer placed each order, you can write the following **INNER JOIN** statement:

SELECT customers.customer_name, orders.order_id, orders.order_date FROM customers INNER JOIN orders ON customers.customer_id = orders.customer_id;

Result:

customer_name	order_id	order_date
Alice	101	2024-09-20
Bob	102	2024-09-21
Alice	103	2024-09-22

With this **INNER JOIN**, you're telling MySQL: "Give me the rows where the customer_id in the customers table matches the customer_id in the orders table."

LEFT JOIN EXAMPLE

Now, let's say you want to see all customers, even if they haven't placed any orders yet. That's when **LEFT JOIN** comes in handy.

SELECT customers.customer_name, orders.order_id, orders.order_date FROM customers LEFT JOIN orders ON customers.customer_id = orders.customer_id;

Result:

customer_name	order_id	order_date
Alice	101	2024-09-20
Bob	102	2024-09-21
Alice	103	2024-09-22
Charlie	NULL	NULL

Notice that **Charlie** appears in the result even though there's no matching order for him. That's the power of a **LEFT JOIN**.

AGGREGATE FUNCTIONS

Alright, now that you have a handle on joining tables, it's time to learn how to **summarize and analyze** your data using **aggregate functions**. These are super useful when you want to get insights from your data, like finding out the total sales, the average order amount, or the number of customers.

WHAT ARE AGGREGATE FUNCTIONS?

Aggregate functions perform a calculation on a set of values and return a **single result**. Instead of getting individual rows back, you'll get a summary. Here are some of the most common aggregate functions:

1. **SUM()**: Adds up all the values in a column.
2. **COUNT()**: Counts the number of rows.
3. **AVG()**: Calculates the average of a set of values.
4. **MIN()**: Finds the smallest value.
5. **MAX()**: Finds the largest value.

Let's go through each one with examples.

SUM()

Let's say you have an orders table that stores the total amount for each order. You want to know how much money you made from all orders.

order_id	customer_id	order_total
101	1	250.00
102	2	150.00
103	1	300.00

To get the total sales, you can use the **SUM()** function:

SELECT SUM(order_total) AS total_sales FROM orders;

Result:

total_sales
700.00

So, the total sales amount from all orders is **$700.00**.

COUNT()

The **COUNT()** function helps you find out how many rows are in a table or how many entries meet a specific condition. For example, let's count how many orders we have:

SELECT COUNT(order_id) AS total_orders FROM orders;

total_orders
3

Now you know there are **3 orders** in your table.

AVG()

What if you want to find out the average value of an order? Use the **AVG()** function:

SELECT AVG(order_total) AS average_order FROM orders;

Result:

average_order
233.33

The average order amount is **$233.33**.

MIN() AND MAX()

These functions help you find the smallest and largest values in a column. For example, to find the smallest and largest order totals, you would use:

SELECT MIN(order_total) AS smallest_order, MAX(order_total) AS largest_order

FROM orders;

Result:

smallest_order	largest_order
150.00	300.00

So, the smallest order was **$150.00**, and the largest was **$300.00**.

COMBINING AGGREGATE FUNCTIONS WITH GROUP BY

You can make aggregate functions even more powerful by combining them with the **GROUP BY** clause. This allows you to group your results by a specific column and then perform the aggregate functions on each group.

For example, if you want to see the total sales per customer, you can write:

SELECT customer_id, SUM(order_total) AS total_sales

FROM orders

GROUP BY customer_id;

Result:

customer_id	total_sales
1	550.00
2	150.00

Now, you can see that **Customer 1** has spent **$550.00** in total, while **Customer 2** has spent **$150.00**.

That's a wrap for aggregate functions! They're super helpful for summarizing data and can save you a lot of time when analyzing information.

GROUP DATA

Now that you're familiar with aggregate functions, it's time to see how you can **group data** to make those functions even more powerful. Grouping allows you to break down your data into smaller chunks, making it easier to analyze trends, patterns, or summaries for specific categories.

WHAT DOES GROUPING DATA MEAN?

Imagine you have a sales report for a company, and you want to know how much each salesperson has sold, or you want to see the total sales per month. To do this, you need to **group** your data based on a certain column. This is where the **GROUP BY** clause comes in.

In simple terms, **GROUP BY** takes your rows and groups them by the values in one or more columns. Then, you can apply aggregate functions to each group separately.

SYNTAX

SELECT column_name, AGGREGATE_FUNCTION(column_name)
FROM table_name
GROUP BY column_name;

EXAMPLE: GROUPING SALES DATA

Let's say you have an orders table that looks like this:

order_id	customer_id	order_total	order_date
101	1	250.00	2024-09-20
102	2	150.00	2024-09-21
103	1	300.00	2024-09-22
104	3	200.00	2024-10-01
105	2	180.00	2024-10-05

If you want to know how much each customer has spent in total, you would write:

```
SELECT customer_id, SUM(order_total) AS total_sales
FROM orders
GROUP BY customer_id;
```

Result:

customer_id	total_sales
1	550.00
2	330.00
3	200.00

Here, **GROUP BY** grouped the rows by customer_id, and **SUM()** calculated the total sales for each customer.

GROUPING BY MULTIPLE COLUMNS

You're not limited to grouping by just one column. You can group by multiple columns to get more specific results.

For example, let's say you want to see the total sales per customer **per month**. You would write:

SELECT customer_id, MONTH(order_date) AS order_month, SUM(order_total) AS total_sales
FROM orders GROUP BY customer_id, MONTH(order_date);

Result:

customer_id	order_month	total_sales
1	9	550.00
2	9	150.00
2	10	180.00
3	10	200.00

Now, you can see how much each customer spent in each month, giving you a more detailed breakdown.

USING GROUP BY WITH HAVING

Sometimes, you might want to filter the groups based on a certain condition. For example, what if you only want to see customers who have spent more than $200? You can't use **WHERE** for this because **WHERE** filters rows before they're grouped. Instead, you use **HAVING** to filter groups after the aggregation.

SELECT customer_id, SUM(order_total) AS total_sales

FROM orders GROUP BY customer_id HAVING total_sales > 200;

Result:

customer_id	total_sales
1	550.00
2	330.00

This query gives you a list of customers who have spent more than $200 in total.

WHY IS GROUPING DATA IMPORTANT?

Grouping data is a key concept when you want to analyze information and spot trends. Whether you're tracking sales performance, monitoring website activity, or even looking at student grades, **GROUP BY** helps you turn rows of data into meaningful summaries.

For example:

- **Sales by product**: Understand which products are performing well.
- **Expenses by category**: Analyze where most of your budget is going.
- **Visitors by region**: Identify your strongest markets.

That's it for grouping data! It's a powerful tool that, when combined with aggregate functions, allows you to get meaningful insights from your datasets.

USING HAVING

In the previous section, we talked about **GROUP BY** and how it allows us to group data for analysis. But what if we want to filter the groups based on the results of an aggregate function? That's where the **HAVING** clause comes into play.

WHAT IS HAVING?

The **HAVING** clause is used to filter groups after they've been created by the **GROUP BY** clause. While the **WHERE** clause filters rows before grouping, **HAVING** allows you to filter groups based on aggregate functions like SUM(), COUNT(), AVG(), and others.

In other words, **HAVING** is like **WHERE** for groups of data.

SYNTAX

SELECT column_name, AGGREGATE_FUNCTION(column_name) FROM table_name GROUP BY column_name HAVING condition;

The **HAVING** clause always comes after the **GROUP BY** clause and is used to apply conditions to the grouped data.

EXAMPLE: FILTERING GROUPS WITH HAVING

Let's use the same orders table from the previous example:

order_id	customer_id	order_total	order_date
101	1	250.00	2024-09-20
102	2	150.00	2024-09-21
103	1	300.00	2024-09-22
104	3	200.00	2024-10-01
105	2	180.00	2024-10-05

Filtering Total Sales

Let's say you want to find out which customers have spent more than $300 in total. You can use the **HAVING** clause to filter those customers:

SELECT customer_id, SUM(order_total) AS total_sales FROM orders GROUP BY customer_id HAVING total_sales > 300;

Result:

customer_id	total_sales
1	550.00
2	330.00

Here, the **HAVING** clause filters out any customers whose total sales are less than or equal to $300. Notice that **HAVING** works with the result of the **SUM()** function.

Why Can't We Use WHERE?

You might be wondering, why can't we use **WHERE** instead of **HAVING**? The reason is that **WHERE** applies **before** the rows are grouped. For instance, in the following query:

SELECT customer_id, SUM(order_total) AS total_sales FROM orders WHERE total_sales > 300 GROUP BY customer_id;

This query will throw an error because **WHERE** tries to filter based on total_sales, which doesn't exist until after the rows have been grouped and summed. **HAVING** solves this problem because it operates after the aggregation.

ANOTHER EXAMPLE: COUNTING ORDERS

Let's say you want to find out which customers have placed more than 1 order. You can use the **COUNT()** function along with **HAVING** to filter those groups:

SELECT customer_id, COUNT(order_id) AS order_count FROM orders GROUP BY customer_id HAVING order_count > 1;

Result:

customer_id order_count

customer_id	order_count
1	2
2	2

This query groups the orders by customer_id, counts how many orders each customer has placed, and then uses **HAVING** to only show customers who have placed more than 1 order.

COMBINING HAVING WITH OTHER CLAUSES

You can combine **HAVING** with other clauses to create even more powerful queries. For example, you can filter rows with **WHERE** and then filter the groups with **HAVING**. Here's an example where we want to see which customers spent more than $200 in orders placed after September 2024:

SELECT customer_id, SUM(order_total) AS total_sales FROM orders WHERE order_date > '2024-09-01' GROUP BY customer_id HAVING total_sales > 200;

Result:

customer_id	total_sales
1	550.00
2	180.00

In this query:

- **WHERE** filters out orders that were placed before September 2024.
- **GROUP BY** groups the remaining orders by customer_id.
- **HAVING** filters out any customers whose total sales are less than $200.

WHY USE HAVING?

The **HAVING** clause is essential when working with aggregate data. It allows you to filter groups based on the results of aggregate functions, giving you more control over the data you analyze. Here are some use cases:

- **Sales analysis**: Find customers or products with total sales over a certain amount.
- **Website traffic**: Identify pages with more than a specific number of visits.
- **Survey results**: Analyze groups of respondents based on their total scores.

And that's how you use **HAVING** to filter grouped data! It's a handy tool to refine your results even further after grouping.

PRIMARY KEYS

When working with databases, one of the most important concepts to understand is **Primary Keys**. Think of them as unique identifiers for records within a table. They play a crucial role in ensuring the integrity of your data, making it easy to locate and reference specific rows.

WHAT IS A PRIMARY KEY?

A **Primary Key** is a column (or a set of columns) in a table that uniquely identifies each row in that table. No two rows can have the same value for the primary key, and a primary key cannot contain NULL values. This ensures that each record is distinct, and there are no duplicates.

WHY IS A PRIMARY KEY IMPORTANT?

1. **Uniqueness**: Each record in a table must be uniquely identifiable, and the primary key ensures this. It's like a national ID number or a passport number; no two people can have the same ID.
2. **Data Integrity**: By enforcing uniqueness, primary keys help maintain data integrity, making sure you don't accidentally insert duplicate records.
3. **Efficient Access**: Primary keys are used to quickly find and retrieve data from a table. They also play a vital role when linking data between multiple tables (more on this later when we discuss Foreign Keys).

EXAMPLE: STUDENT TABLE

Let's take a look at an example:

student_id	first_name	last_name	age
1	John	Doe	20
2	Jane	Smith	22
3	Mike	Johnson	21

In this **students** table, the student_id column serves as the primary key. Each student has a unique ID, and no two rows can have the same student_id. If someone tries to insert a record with an existing student_id, the database will throw an error.

CREATING A PRIMARY KEY

When creating a new table, you can define a primary key like this:

```
CREATE TABLE students (
    student_id INT PRIMARY KEY,
    first_name VARCHAR(50),
    last_name VARCHAR(50),
    age INT
);
```

In the example above, the student_id column is declared as the **Primary Key**. This ensures:

- Each value in student_id must be unique.
- No NULL values can be entered in student_id.

AUTO_INCREMENT PRIMARY KEYS

In many cases, especially when dealing with IDs, you might not want to manually assign a unique value each time you insert a new record. That's where **AUTO_INCREMENT** comes in handy.

Here's an example:

```
CREATE TABLE employees (
    employee_id INT AUTO_INCREMENT PRIMARY KEY,
    first_name VARCHAR(50),
    last_name VARCHAR(50),
    position VARCHAR(50)
);
```

With **AUTO_INCREMENT**, every time you add a new row to the **employees** table, the employee_id will automatically be assigned a unique, incrementing number.

MODIFYING AN EXISTING TABLE TO ADD A PRIMARY KEY

If you already have a table and want to add a primary key to it, you can use the **ALTER TABLE** statement:

```
ALTER TABLE students
ADD PRIMARY KEY (student_id);
```

Just make sure that the student_id column has unique values before you try to set it as a primary key.

COMPOSITE PRIMARY KEYS

Sometimes, a single column is not enough to uniquely identify each row. In such cases, you can use a **Composite Primary Key**, which is a primary key made up of two or more columns.

EXAMPLE: ORDER ITEMS TABLE

Let's say you have a table that stores the items in customer orders:

order_id	product_id	quantity
101	1	2
101	2	1
102	3	4

In this table, neither order_id nor product_id alone can uniquely identify each row, but together they can. You can create a composite primary key like this:

```
CREATE TABLE order_items (
    order_id INT,
    product_id INT,
    quantity INT,
    PRIMARY KEY (order_id, product_id)
);
```

Why Use Composite Keys?

- **More Detailed Uniqueness**: Composite keys can be useful when the combination of multiple columns is needed to ensure uniqueness. For example, one order can have multiple products, but each product within the same order is unique.

- **Data Relationships**: Composite keys can help establish more complex relationships in the database, especially when you start connecting multiple tables.

PRIMARY KEYS AND DATA RELATIONSHIPS

Primary keys are not just about keeping rows unique; they are essential for establishing relationships between different tables. For example, in a **one-to-many** relationship, the primary key from one table can be used as a **foreign key** in another. This allows you to efficiently link records across multiple tables, which is fundamental for complex databases.

BEST PRACTICES FOR PRIMARY KEYS

1. **Use Meaningless Keys**: When possible, use an auto-generated numeric ID as a primary key instead of something meaningful, like a name or code. This helps avoid issues when the meaning of the data changes over time.
2. **Keep It Simple**: Try to avoid composite keys unless necessary. A single-column primary key is easier to manage and understand.
3. **Ensure Uniqueness and Non-NULL**: Always make sure your primary key column is set up to enforce uniqueness and doesn't allow NULL values.

Now you have a solid understanding of **Primary Keys** and why they are essential to any relational database. They help keep your data accurate, organized, and easy to retrieve. In the next section, we'll discuss **Foreign Keys**, which will show you how to connect data between different tables. Keep going—you're building a strong foundation in SQL!

FOREIGN KEYS

Now that we have discussed **primary keys**, let's explore another fundamental concept: **foreign keys**. Foreign keys are essential for establishing relationships between tables in a database, allowing data to be organized efficiently and coherently.

WHAT IS A FOREIGN KEY?

A **foreign key** is a column or a set of columns in one table that references the primary key of another table. This creates a link between the two tables, allowing you to connect records in a meaningful way.

WHY ARE FOREIGN KEYS IMPORTANT?

1. **Referential Integrity**: Foreign keys ensure that relationships between tables remain consistent. If a record in the referenced table (the table containing the primary key) is deleted or modified, the foreign key ensures that the related records in the dependent table do not become "orphans."
2. **Data Organization**: Foreign keys help keep data organized, enabling you to avoid duplicating information and maintain a normalized database.
3. **Related Queries**: With foreign keys, you can efficiently perform queries involving multiple tables, using JOINs to combine data based on the defined relationships.

EXAMPLE: STUDENTS AND COURSES TABLES

Let's consider an example with two tables: **students** and **courses**.

Students Table

student_id	name
1	John Doe
2	Jane Smith
3	Mike Johnson

Courses Table

course_id	course_name
101	Mathematics
102	History
103	Science

Now, suppose we want to create a **registrations** table that links students to courses. This table will have a foreign key referencing both the **students** and **courses** tables.

Registrations Table

registration_id	student_id	course_id
1	1	101
2	2	102
3	3	103

Here, the student_id and course_id columns in the **registrations** table are foreign keys that reference student_id in the **students** table and course_id in the **courses** table, respectively.

HOW TO CREATE A FOREIGN KEY

To create a foreign key, you can define it while creating the table using the following syntax:

```
CREATE TABLE registrations (
    registration_id INT PRIMARY KEY,
    student_id INT,
    course_id INT,
    FOREIGN        KEY        (student_id)        REFERENCES
students(student_id),
    FOREIGN KEY (course_id) REFERENCES courses(course_id)
);
```

CODE EXPLANATION:

- **FOREIGN   KEY   (student_id)   REFERENCES students(student_id)**: This line defines student_id as a foreign key that references the student_id column in the **students** table.
- **FOREIGN   KEY   (course_id)   REFERENCES courses(course_id)**: This line defines course_id as a foreign key that references the course_id column in the **courses** table.

FOREIGN KEY CONSTRAINTS

Foreign keys can be configured with some options, such as:

1. **ON DELETE CASCADE**: If a record in the referenced table is deleted, all related records in the dependent table will also be deleted automatically.
2. **ON UPDATE CASCADE**: If the primary key in the referenced table is updated, the corresponding foreign key in the dependent table will be automatically updated.

CONSTRAINT EXAMPLE

```
CREATE TABLE registrations (
    registration_id INT PRIMARY KEY,
    student_id INT,
    course_id INT,
    FOREIGN KEY (student_id) REFERENCES students(student_id)
ON DELETE CASCADE,
    FOREIGN KEY (course_id) REFERENCES courses(course_id)
ON UPDATE CASCADE
);
```

BEST PRACTICES FOR FOREIGN KEYS

1. **Consistent Naming**: Use descriptive names for your foreign keys to make it easier to identify relationships.
2. **Maintain Integrity**: Whenever possible, use foreign keys to enforce referential integrity in your database.
3. **Plan Relationships**: Before creating your tables, think through the relationships between the data so that you can effectively design your primary and foreign keys.

Now you understand what **Foreign Keys** are, how they work, and why they are essential for relationships between tables in a MySQL database. In the next chapter, we will discuss **Indexes**, which help improve the performance of your queries. Let's keep going!

INDEXES

As your database grows, you might notice that searching for data becomes slower. That's where **indexes** come into play. Indexes are a powerful tool for optimizing database performance, especially when dealing with large volumes of data.

WHAT IS AN INDEX?

An **index** is a data structure that improves the speed of data retrieval operations on a table. Think of it as a book's index; instead of scanning the entire book to find a specific topic, you can quickly locate the right page using the index.

Without an index, MySQL must scan every row in a table to find the desired result. With an index, MySQL can jump directly to where the data is stored, making queries much faster.

HOW DOES AN INDEX WORK?

When you create an index on a column, MySQL builds a data structure that stores the values of that column along with pointers to the actual rows. When you search for a specific value, MySQL uses the index to quickly locate the data instead of scanning the entire table.

CREATING AN INDEX

You can create an index using the following syntax:

CREATE INDEX index_name ON table_name (column_name);

EXAMPLE

Let's say you have a **customers** table:

customer_id	name	email
1	John Doe	john@example.com
2	Jane Smith	jane@example.com
3	Mike Johnson	mike@example.com

If you often search for customers by their email, you can create an index on the email column:

CREATE INDEX idx_email ON customers (email);

Now, whenever you run a query to find a customer by email, MySQL will use the index to speed up the search:

SELECT * FROM customers WHERE email = 'john@example.com';

TYPES OF INDEXES IN MYSQL

MySQL supports several types of indexes:

1. **PRIMARY INDEX**: Created automatically when you define a primary key on a table. Ensures that each value in the primary key column is unique.
2. **UNIQUE INDEX**: Similar to the primary index, but it can be created on any column. It prevents duplicate values in the indexed column.

CREATE UNIQUE INDEX idx_unique_email ON customers (email);

3. **FULLTEXT INDEX**: Used for searching text columns. It's particularly useful for text-heavy data, such as searching within product descriptions or blog posts.

CREATE FULLTEXT INDEX idx_fulltext ON products (description);

4. **COMPOSITE INDEX**: An index that includes multiple columns. Useful when you frequently search for a combination of values.

CREATE INDEX idx_composite ON orders (customer_id, order_date);

WHEN TO USE INDEXES

Indexes are incredibly useful, but they should be used wisely. Here are a few best practices:

1. **Index Frequently Queried Columns**: If you often search or filter data by a particular column, create an index for it. For example, columns used in WHERE, JOIN, and ORDER BY clauses are good candidates.
2. **Limit the Number of Indexes**: While indexes speed up data retrieval, they can slow down INSERT, UPDATE, and DELETE operations. Each time data is modified, MySQL must also update the indexes, which can impact performance.
3. **Use Composite Indexes Carefully**: Only create composite indexes if you frequently query by multiple columns together. MySQL can use the composite index if you query with the leftmost columns in the index.

CHECKING INDEXES

To check the indexes on a table, you can use the SHOW INDEX command:

SHOW INDEX FROM customers;

This will display information about all the indexes on the **customers** table, including their names, columns, and types.

REMOVING AN INDEX

If you no longer need an index, you can remove it using the DROP INDEX statement:

DROP INDEX idx_email ON customers;

IMPORTANT: USE INDEXES WISELY

Indexes are a powerful tool for improving database performance, but they come with trade-offs. They speed up SELECT queries but can slow down INSERT, UPDATE, and DELETE operations. Always consider the overall usage of your database when deciding which columns to index.

With this understanding of **indexes**, you can now make your MySQL database faster and more efficient.

USING COMMENTS

When writing SQL code, it's essential to make your queries clear and understandable, especially if you plan to revisit them later or if someone else will be reading your code. One way to achieve this is by using **comments**.

Comments are lines in your SQL code that are ignored by the MySQL server. They are meant solely for the reader of the code, to explain what the code does, why certain decisions were made, or to provide any other helpful context. Comments can make your code more readable and maintainable.

TYPES OF COMMENTS IN MYSQL

MySQL supports three types of comments:

1. SINGLE-LINE COMMENTS

Single-line comments begin with -- (two hyphens) or # (a hash symbol). Anything that follows on the same line will be treated as a comment and ignored by MySQL.

Using -- for single-line comments:

```
-- This query retrieves all records from the customers table
SELECT * FROM customers;
```

Using # for single-line comments:

```
# This query deletes a customer with the ID 5
DELETE FROM customers WHERE customer_id = 5;
```

2. MULTI-LINE COMMENTS

If you need to write a comment that spans multiple lines, you can use the /* */ syntax. Everything between /* and */ is treated as a comment, allowing you to write detailed explanations.

Example of multi-line comment:

```
/*
This query calculates the total sales for each customer.
We are using a JOIN to combine the customers and orders tables,
and GROUP BY to aggregate the results.
*/
SELECT customers.customer_id, SUM(orders.total_amount) AS
total_sales
```

```
FROM customers
JOIN orders ON customers.customer_id = orders.customer_id
GROUP BY customers.customer_id;
```

WHY USE COMMENTS?

1.

Make Code More Understandable: Explaining what a query does can help others (or even yourself) understand it when you return to it later.

```
-- Fetch all customers who placed an order in the last 30 days

SELECT * FROM customers WHERE last_order_date >=
CURDATE() - INTERVAL 30 DAY;
```

Explain Complex Logic: If your query involves complex joins, subqueries, or calculations, comments can clarify your thought process.

```
/*
```

This query identifies customers who haven't placed an order in over a year.

We are using a LEFT JOIN to find those with no orders in the last 12 months.

```
*/

SELECT customers.name
```

FROM customers

LEFT JOIN orders ON customers.customer_id = orders.customer_id

WHERE orders.order_date < CURDATE() - INTERVAL 1 YEAR OR orders.order_date IS NULL;

Mark Sections of Code: When writing longer SQL scripts, comments can help organize your code by marking different sections. This is especially useful for stored procedures and scripts that contain multiple operations.

-- STEP 1: Create temporary table to store intermediate results

CREATE TEMPORARY TABLE temp_sales AS

SELECT * FROM sales WHERE sale_date > '2024-01-01';

-- STEP 2: Aggregate results and insert into the final table

INSERT INTO annual_sales (year, total_sales)

SELECT YEAR(sale_date), SUM(amount)

FROM temp_sales

GROUP BY YEAR(sale_date);

BEST PRACTICES FOR USING COMMENTS

1. **Be Concise**: Write comments that are short but descriptive. Avoid over-explaining simple queries, but ensure that complex logic is well-documented.
2. **Update Comments as Code Changes**: If your query changes, make sure to update the corresponding comments. Outdated comments can cause confusion.
3. **Use Comments to Explain the Why, Not Just the What**: It's often clear what a query does by reading the SQL itself. Use comments to explain why you're doing something a particular way, especially if it's not immediately obvious.

WHEN NOT TO USE COMMENTS

Avoid Obvious Comments: If the query is self-explanatory, you don't need a comment. For instance, a query like SELECT * FROM products; doesn't need a comment saying "Select all products."

Don't Overuse Comments: While comments are helpful, too many can make the code cluttered. Use them judiciously to avoid overwhelming the reader.

By using comments effectively, you can make your SQL scripts more readable and maintainable. It's a small step that can have a big impact, especially when working on larger projects or in a team setting.

TRANSACTIONS

In MySQL, a **transaction** is a sequence of one or more SQL statements that are executed as a single unit of work. Transactions are essential when you need to ensure that a group of operations is either fully completed or not executed at all. This is crucial for maintaining data integrity, especially when dealing with complex operations like transferring funds, updating multiple records, or any operation that requires atomicity.

WHY USE TRANSACTIONS?

Imagine you're building a banking system, and you need to transfer $500 from Account A to Account B. This operation involves two key actions:

1. Deduct $500 from Account A.
2. Add $500 to Account B.

If one of these actions fails (for instance, if the system crashes after deducting the money but before adding it), your data would be inconsistent. Account A would have lost $500, but Account B would not have received it. By using transactions, you can ensure that both actions are completed, or none are—keeping the data consistent.

ACID PROPERTIES

Transactions follow four main properties, known as **ACID**:

1. **Atomicity**: Ensures that all the operations within a transaction are treated as a single unit. If one

operation fails, the entire transaction fails, and any changes are rolled back.

2. **Consistency**: Guarantees that a transaction will bring the database from one valid state to another, preserving data integrity.
3. **Isolation**: Ensures that transactions are isolated from one another. The operations within a transaction are not visible to other transactions until the transaction is completed.
4. **Durability**: Once a transaction is committed, the changes are permanent, even in the case of a system crash.

USING TRANSACTIONS IN MYSQL

BEGINNING AND ENDING A TRANSACTION

To use transactions in MySQL, you need to know three main commands:

- **START TRANSACTION**: Begins a new transaction.
- **COMMIT**: Saves the changes made during the transaction permanently.
- **ROLLBACK**: Reverts any changes made during the transaction, effectively canceling it.

EXAMPLE OF A TRANSACTION

Here's a simple example that demonstrates how to use transactions to transfer funds between two accounts:

```
START TRANSACTION;

-- Deduct $500 from Account A

UPDATE accounts

SET balance = balance - 500

WHERE account_id = 'A';


-- Add $500 to Account B

UPDATE accounts

SET balance = balance + 500

WHERE account_id = 'B';


-- Save the changes

COMMIT;
```

In this example:

1. The START TRANSACTION command begins the transaction.

2. Two UPDATE statements deduct $500 from Account A and add $500 to Account B.
3. The COMMIT command finalizes the transaction and saves the changes.

ROLLING BACK A TRANSACTION

If something goes wrong while executing a transaction, you can use ROLLBACK to undo the changes:

START TRANSACTION;

UPDATE accounts

SET balance = balance - 500

WHERE account_id = 'A';

-- Suppose an error occurs here

UPDATE accounts

SET balance = balance + 500

WHERE account_id = 'B';

-- Cancel the transaction

ROLLBACK;

In this case, even if the first UPDATE statement succeeds, the ROLLBACK command will revert it if the second UPDATE fails, ensuring no funds are lost.

AUTOCOMMIT MODE

By default, MySQL operates in **autocommit mode**, meaning that every individual statement is treated as a transaction and automatically committed once it's executed. If you want to use transactions, you need to turn off autocommit:

SET autocommit = 0;

-- Start your transaction here

START TRANSACTION;

When you're done, you can turn it back on:

SET autocommit = 1;

SAVEPOINTS: PARTIAL ROLLBACKS

Sometimes, you may want to roll back to a specific point within a transaction without canceling the entire transaction. You can do this using **SAVEPOINTS**:

START TRANSACTION;

```
-- Create a savepoint

SAVEPOINT step1;


UPDATE accounts

SET balance = balance - 500

WHERE account_id = 'A';


-- Something goes wrong, revert to step1

ROLLBACK TO step1;


-- Continue the transaction

COMMIT;
```

In this example, if an error occurs, the ROLLBACK TO step1 command will undo everything after the savepoint, but it won't cancel the entire transaction.

BEST PRACTICES FOR TRANSACTIONS

1. **Keep Transactions Short**: The longer a transaction is open, the higher the chances of locking resources and

causing delays. Keep your transactions short and to the point.
2. **Handle Errors Gracefully**: Always prepare for possible errors by using ROLLBACK and handling exceptions properly.
3. **Be Careful with Autocommit**: If you need to group multiple operations, make sure to disable autocommit, so you can control when to save or discard changes.

Transactions are an essential part of managing data in MySQL. They allow you to maintain data integrity and ensure that all operations are performed successfully or not at all.

Next, we will look at **Stored Procedures**, which help you bundle your SQL code into reusable routines.

STORED PROCEDURES

In MySQL, a **stored procedure** is a set of SQL statements that you can save and reuse. It allows you to encapsulate and organize frequently-used operations into a single, callable unit. This is particularly useful for repetitive tasks, complex queries, and maintaining a consistent logic across your applications. Stored procedures can help improve efficiency and code reusability, and they can also improve performance by reducing the need to send multiple queries from an application.

WHY USE STORED PROCEDURES?

Stored procedures provide several benefits:

1. **Reusability**: Instead of writing the same SQL queries over and over again, you can just call the stored procedure.
2. **Maintainability**: Changes to business logic are easier to implement, as you only need to modify the procedure in one place.
3. **Security**: You can control access by granting permission to execute the procedure without giving users direct access to the underlying tables.
4. **Performance**: Reduces network traffic between your application and the database because multiple operations are executed on the server with a single call.

CREATING A STORED PROCEDURE

To create a stored procedure in MySQL, you use the CREATE PROCEDURE statement. Here's a simple example:

DELIMITER //

CREATE PROCEDURE GetCustomerOrders (IN customerId INT)

BEGIN

   SELECT order_id, order_date, total_amount

   FROM orders

   WHERE customer_id = customerId;

END //

DELIMITER ;

EXPLANATION

1. **DELIMITER**: By default, MySQL treats ; as the end of a statement. Since a procedure contains multiple statements, you need to temporarily change the delimiter so MySQL knows when the procedure definition ends. In this case, we use //.
2. **CREATE PROCEDURE**: This creates a new stored procedure named GetCustomerOrders.
3. **IN customerId INT**: Defines an input parameter, customerId, that the procedure will use.
4. **BEGIN...END**: Encloses the procedure's statements. Here, the SELECT query retrieves orders for a specific customer.

After creating the procedure, you can call it like this:

CALL GetCustomerOrders(1);

INPUT AND OUTPUT PARAMETERS

Stored procedures can accept **input parameters** (IN), **output parameters** (OUT), and **input/output parameters** (INOUT). Here's how they work:

- **IN**: Passes a value into the procedure. The procedure can use the value but doesn't change it outside of the procedure.
- **OUT**: Passes a value back from the procedure to the caller.
- **INOUT**: Can be used both to pass a value in and receive a modified value back.

EXAMPLE WITH INPUT AND OUTPUT PARAMETERS

DELIMITER //

CREATE PROCEDURE UpdateProductPrice (IN productId INT, IN newPrice DECIMAL(10,2), OUT successMessage VARCHAR(100))

BEGIN

  UPDATE products

  SET price = newPrice

  WHERE id = productId;

  SET successMessage = 'Price updated successfully!';

END //

DELIMITER ;

To call this procedure and capture the output:

CALL UpdateProductPrice(1, 19.99, @message);

SELECT @message;

In this example, the OUT parameter successMessage returns a string that tells us whether the operation was successful.

MODIFYING AND DELETING PROCEDURES

If you need to change an existing stored procedure, you will have to **drop** it first and then recreate it:

DROP PROCEDURE

DROP PROCEDURE IF EXISTS GetCustomerOrders;

RE-CREATE THE PROCEDURE

After dropping it, you can recreate the procedure with your modifications.

BEST PRACTICES FOR USING STORED PROCEDURES

1. **Error Handling**: Always include proper error handling mechanisms in your procedures. You can use DECLARE statements to handle conditions and errors.
2. **Keep It Simple**: Avoid overly complex procedures. If a procedure is getting too long or complicated, consider breaking it into smaller ones.

3. **Use Comments**: Include comments within your procedures to explain what each section does. This makes it easier for others to understand your code.
4. **Security**: Limit the permissions granted to users. If they only need to execute a procedure, give them permission to call the procedure but not to modify the tables directly.

EXAMPLE OF ERROR HANDLING

```
DELIMITER //


CREATE PROCEDURE SafeTransfer (IN fromAccount INT, IN toAccount INT, IN amount DECIMAL(10,2))

BEGIN

  DECLARE EXIT HANDLER FOR SQLEXCEPTION

  BEGIN

    ROLLBACK;

    SELECT 'An error occurred, transaction rolled back.' AS message;

  END;


  START TRANSACTION;
```

```
UPDATE accounts

SET balance = balance - amount

WHERE account_id = fromAccount;


UPDATE accounts

SET balance = balance + amount

WHERE account_id = toAccount;


COMMIT;

END //


DELIMITER ;
```

In this example, if any of the UPDATE statements fail, the EXIT HANDLER triggers a rollback, ensuring no partial updates are left.

Stored procedures are a powerful way to encapsulate and reuse SQL logic. They help streamline your code, making it more maintainable, secure, and efficient. As you become more comfortable with MySQL, stored procedures will become essential for optimizing your workflow and ensuring consistent operations across your applications.

Next, let's move on to **Triggers**—another advanced feature that can help automate tasks in your database.

TRIGGERS

In MySQL, a **trigger** is a set of SQL statements that automatically execute in response to certain events on a table. Triggers can be set to run before or after data modifications, such as **INSERT**, **UPDATE**, or **DELETE** operations. They are useful for enforcing business rules, maintaining data integrity, and automating tasks within the database.

WHY USE TRIGGERS?

Triggers can be beneficial in several ways:

1. **Data Integrity**: Automatically enforce rules and ensure consistent data by checking conditions before allowing changes.
2. **Auditing**: Track changes by logging updates, deletions, or insertions to another table, creating a history of modifications.
3. **Automation**: Automate repetitive tasks, such as updating related tables when certain changes occur.

CREATING TRIGGERS

To create a trigger, use the CREATE TRIGGER statement. A trigger must be associated with a table, and you need to specify when it should run (either **BEFORE** or **AFTER** a specified event).

EXAMPLE: BEFORE INSERT

Suppose we have a table called employees and we want to automatically set a default created_at timestamp before a new record is inserted. We can use a trigger like this:

CREATE TRIGGER before_employee_insert

BEFORE INSERT ON employees

FOR EACH ROW

BEGIN

   SET NEW.created_at = NOW();

END;

EXPLANATION:

1. **CREATE TRIGGER**: Defines a new trigger named before_employee_insert.
2. **BEFORE INSERT**: Specifies that this trigger should run before a new row is inserted into the employees table.
3. **FOR EACH ROW**: Ensures that the trigger runs for every row being inserted.

4. **NEW**: Refers to the new row that is about to be inserted. In this case, NEW.created_at sets the timestamp before the row is saved.

EXAMPLE: AFTER UPDATE

Let's say we have an orders table, and every time an order is updated, we want to record the update in an order_log table. Here's how you could set up an AFTER UPDATE trigger:

CREATE TRIGGER after_order_update

AFTER UPDATE ON orders

FOR EACH ROW

BEGIN

   INSERT INTO order_log (order_id, change_date, old_status, new_status)

   VALUES (OLD.id, NOW(), OLD.status, NEW.status);

END;

EXPLANATION:

1. **AFTER UPDATE**: Specifies that this trigger should run after an UPDATE operation on the orders table.
2. **OLD** and **NEW**: OLD refers to the existing row data before the update, while NEW refers to the row data after the update. This allows you to capture and compare changes.

3. **INSERT INTO order_log**: Saves the changes into a log table, creating a record of each update.

DROPPING TRIGGERS

If you need to remove a trigger, use the DROP TRIGGER statement:

DROP TRIGGER IF EXISTS before_employee_insert;

This command deletes the before_employee_insert trigger, if it exists, from the database.

BEST PRACTICES FOR USING TRIGGERS

1. **Avoid Complex Logic**: While triggers are powerful, they can quickly become difficult to maintain if they contain complex logic. Keep triggers simple and focused on a single task.
2. **Be Mindful of Performance**: Triggers run automatically and can impact performance if they contain heavy queries. Use them only when necessary and optimize the queries within the trigger.
3. **Consider Order of Execution**: MySQL processes BEFORE triggers before the operation and AFTER triggers afterward. Be aware of this order when designing triggers.
4. **Document Your Triggers**: Since triggers execute in the background, it's important to document what each trigger does so other developers (and your future self) can understand its purpose.

111

EXAMPLE: AUTOMATED BACKUP OF DELETED RECORDS

Here's an example of how you can use a BEFORE DELETE trigger to back up a record before it is deleted:

CREATE TRIGGER before_employee_delete

BEFORE DELETE ON employees

FOR EACH ROW

BEGIN

  INSERT INTO employee_backup (id, name, position, deleted_at)

  VALUES (OLD.id, OLD.name, OLD.position, NOW());

END;

This trigger will save the data of an employee to the employee_backup table before it is deleted from the employees table, ensuring that no data is permanently lost without a backup.

Triggers provide a powerful mechanism to automate tasks, enforce rules, and maintain data integrity in your MySQL databases. However, they should be used carefully to avoid unintended side effects and performance issues.

VIEWS

In MySQL, a **view** is a virtual table that is based on the result set of a query. Unlike a physical table, a view does not store data itself; instead, it dynamically displays data from one or more tables. Views can simplify the way you interact with data by providing a specific perspective of your data, and they are useful for encapsulating complex queries, securing sensitive information, and organizing data access.

WHY USE VIEWS?

Views can be extremely beneficial for several reasons:

1. **Simplify Complex Queries**: If you need to use a complex query frequently, you can save it as a view and simply query the view instead. This makes your SQL code cleaner and easier to manage.
2. **Security**: Views can help you control access to data. For example, if you don't want users to see certain columns, you can create a view that excludes those columns, giving them limited access without revealing sensitive information.
3. **Data Abstraction**: Views allow you to present data in a way that makes sense to different parts of your application, without altering the underlying table structures.

CREATING VIEWS

To create a view, use the CREATE VIEW statement followed by the name you want to give to the view and the query that defines it. Here's a basic example:

EXAMPLE

Suppose you have an employees table with several columns, but you only want to show a few of them in a simplified view:

CREATE VIEW employee_summary AS

SELECT id, name, position

FROM employees;

EXPLANATION:

1. **CREATE VIEW employee_summary**: This command creates a new view named employee_summary.
2. **AS SELECT id, name, position FROM employees**: The view will include only the id, name, and position columns from the employees table. Whenever you query employee_summary, it will return the results of this query.

USING VIEWS

Once a view is created, you can query it just like a regular table:

SELECT * FROM employee_summary;

This command will return a list of employees with only their ID, name, and position, as defined by the view.

UPDATING VIEWS

You can modify an existing view using the ALTER VIEW or CREATE OR REPLACE VIEW statements. For instance, if you want to change the employee_summary view to include the department column, you can do:

CREATE OR REPLACE VIEW employee_summary AS

SELECT id, name, position, department

FROM employees;

This command will update the existing view, adding the department column.

DROPPING VIEWS

If you need to remove a view, you can use the DROP VIEW statement:

DROP VIEW IF EXISTS employee_summary;

This command deletes the employee_summary view if it exists, without affecting the underlying employees table.

BEST PRACTICES FOR USING VIEWS

1. **Keep Views Simple**: While you can create complex queries within views, simpler views are easier to maintain and troubleshoot. Consider creating multiple simpler views if your query logic is too complex.
2. **Use Views for Security**: If certain users should not see specific data, create views to hide that information, giving them controlled access.
3. **Be Mindful of Performance**: Although views are virtual, complex views can slow down query performance, especially when they involve multiple tables with joins or aggregations. Test your views to ensure they do not impact your database's efficiency.
4. **Document Your Views**: Since views provide an abstraction layer, it's essential to document what each view does and why it exists. This helps other developers (and yourself) understand its purpose later.

EXAMPLE: CREATING A VIEW WITH AGGREGATE DATA

You can also use views to simplify access to aggregated data. For example, let's say you want a view that shows the total sales per product:

CREATE VIEW total_sales AS

SELECT product_id, SUM(sales_amount) AS total_sales

FROM sales

GROUP BY product_id;

Now, if you query total_sales, you will see the total sales for each product, without needing to write the GROUP BY query every time.

Views provide a flexible way to manage and present data in your MySQL database. They can simplify complex queries, restrict data access, and help organize your data efficiently.

DATA TYPES CHOICE

When creating tables in MySQL, one of the critical decisions you'll make is choosing the appropriate data types for each column. Selecting the right data type ensures efficient storage, faster query performance, and data integrity. Data types define the kind of data that can be stored in a column, such as numbers, text, dates, and more. MySQL offers a variety of data types, and understanding them will help you make the best decisions for your database.

WHY IS DATA TYPE CHOICE IMPORTANT?

1. **Storage Efficiency**: Using the right data type minimizes the amount of storage space each row takes up. For instance, using INT instead of BIGINT when you only need small numbers can save significant storage space.
2. **Performance**: Smaller data types often result in faster query execution, as less data needs to be read from the disk.
3. **Data Integrity**: Choosing the correct data type ensures that only valid data can be entered. For example, a

column defined as DATE will only accept valid dates, reducing data entry errors.

4. **Functionality**: Some MySQL functions only work with certain data types. Choosing the right type enables you to take full advantage of MySQL's functionality.

COMMON DATA TYPES IN MYSQL

NUMERIC DATA TYPES

INT, SMALLINT, TINYINT, BIGINT: Used for storing integer values.

Use INT for general-purpose numbers.

SMALLINT and TINYINT use less space and are good for smaller numbers.

BIGINT is for very large integers.

DECIMAL, FLOAT, DOUBLE: For storing numbers with decimal points.

Use DECIMAL for exact numeric values, like financial data, where precision matters.

FLOAT and DOUBLE are used for approximate values, typically when you need to save space and exact precision isn't critical.

BOOLEAN: MySQL interprets TINYINT(1) as a boolean value, where 0 means FALSE and 1 means TRUE.

STRING DATA TYPES

CHAR and VARCHAR: For storing text.

CHAR is a fixed-length string, ideal when all entries have the same length.

VARCHAR is a variable-length string, suitable when text length varies.

TEXT, TINYTEXT, MEDIUMTEXT, LONGTEXT: For storing longer pieces of text.

Use TEXT types when you need to store larger blocks of text, like descriptions or articles.

TINYTEXT and LONGTEXT are variations that allow different maximum lengths.

ENUM: Useful for storing a predefined list of values, like ('small', 'medium', 'large').

DATE AND TIME DATA TYPES

1. **DATE**: Stores dates in YYYY-MM-DD format.
2. **TIME**: Stores time in HH:MM:SS format.
3. **DATETIME**: Combines DATE and TIME into a single field, storing date and time.
4. **TIMESTAMP**: Similar to DATETIME but also stores timezone information and automatically updates to the current date and time on certain operations.
5. **YEAR**: Stores a year in a two- or four-digit format, useful when only the year is needed.

SPATIAL DATA TYPES

GEOMETRY, POINT, LINESTRING, POLYGON: These types are used to store spatial or geographical data. Useful when working with map coordinates or geographical locations.

CHOOSING THE RIGHT DATA TYPE

Assess Your Data Needs: Consider the kind of data you expect to store in the column. Will it be whole numbers, decimals, text, or dates? Make your choice accordingly.

Plan for the Future: Choose a data type that accommodates potential future growth. For example, if you expect your IDs to exceed 2 billion, use BIGINT instead of INT.

Balance Precision and Space: If you need to store decimal numbers, ask yourself whether exact precision is critical. If yes, use DECIMAL. Otherwise, use FLOAT or DOUBLE to save space.

Use ENUM for Fixed Values: When you have a column that should only accept a few specific values, ENUM is a perfect choice. It reduces storage and increases data integrity.

EXAMPLE OF A GOOD DATA TYPE CHOICE

Suppose you are creating a products table for an e-commerce platform:

CREATE TABLE products (

```
product_id INT UNSIGNED AUTO_INCREMENT PRIMARY KEY,

name VARCHAR(100) NOT NULL,

description TEXT,

price DECIMAL(10,2) NOT NULL,

stock_quantity SMALLINT UNSIGNED NOT NULL,

created_at DATETIME DEFAULT CURRENT_TIMESTAMP
);
```

Explanation:

- product_id: Using INT UNSIGNED because IDs are always positive and AUTO_INCREMENT to auto-generate new IDs.
- name: Using VARCHAR(100) because product names are variable in length but unlikely to exceed 100 characters.
- description: Using TEXT to store longer product descriptions.
- price: Using DECIMAL(10,2) to ensure exact storage of currency values.
- stock_quantity: Using SMALLINT UNSIGNED because the stock count is positive and a smaller data type saves space.
- created_at: Using DATETIME to record the exact date and time when a product was added.

Selecting the right data types is essential for efficient and effective database design. Make these decisions carefully to ensure your tables are optimized for performance, data integrity, and scalability.

NORMALIZATION

When designing a database, one of the most important concepts to understand is **Normalization**. Normalization is the process of organizing your database tables in such a way that reduces redundancy and improves data integrity. It ensures that data is stored efficiently, making your database more flexible and easier to maintain.

Think of normalization as cleaning up your database to make sure everything is in the right place, just like organizing a bookshelf by genre, author, and title. This helps you find books (or, in this case, data) faster and ensures there are no duplicates.

WHY IS NORMALIZATION IMPORTANT?

1. **Eliminates Redundancy**: Redundant data means having the same information stored in multiple places. This can lead to inconsistencies when one copy is updated but the others are not. Normalization reduces duplication, saving storage and preventing data anomalies.
2. **Improves Data Integrity**: Normalization helps maintain the accuracy and consistency of data. By breaking down data into smaller, related tables, updates become simpler and less error-prone.

3. **Optimizes Performance**: Well-normalized databases generally perform better because they avoid unnecessary repetitions and make better use of indexing.

NORMAL FORMS

Normalization is achieved through a series of **normal forms**, which are rules to organize tables. Let's briefly discuss the most common ones:

FIRST NORMAL FORM (1NF)

1NF ensures that each column contains atomic (indivisible) values, and there are no repeating groups of columns. In other words:

- Each column must contain only one value, not a list.
- Each entry in a column must be of the same data type.

Example: Suppose you have the following table:

OrderID	CustomerName	Items
1	John Doe	Pen, Notebook
2	Jane Smith	Pencil, Eraser

This table violates 1NF because the Items column has multiple values. To make it 1NF compliant, you would split the data:

OrderID	CustomerName	Item
1	John Doe	Pen
1	John Doe	Notebook

OrderID CustomerName Item

| 2 | Jane Smith | Pencil |
| 2 | Jane Smith | Eraser |

SECOND NORMAL FORM (2NF)

2NF requires the table to be in 1NF, and it eliminates partial dependencies. This means that all non-key columns must depend on the entire primary key, not just part of it. This applies mainly to tables with a composite primary key.

Example: Suppose you have a table that looks like this:

OrderID ProductID ProductName CustomerName

| 1 | 101 | Pen | John Doe |
| 2 | 102 | Pencil | Jane Smith |

The ProductName column depends only on ProductID and not on the entire OrderID and ProductID composite key, violating 2NF. To make this 2NF compliant, you would split it into two tables:

Orders Table:

OrderID CustomerName

| 1 | John Doe |
| 2 | Jane Smith |

Products Table:

ProductID ProductName

| 101 | Pen |

ProductID	ProductName
102	Pencil

THIRD NORMAL FORM (3NF)

3NF requires that the table be in 2NF, and it eliminates transitive dependencies. This means that non-key columns must depend only on the primary key and not on other non-key columns.

Example: Suppose you have this table:

ProductID	ProductName	SupplierName	SupplierCity
101	Pen	OfficeGoods	New York
102	Pencil	OfficeGoods	New York

The SupplierCity depends on SupplierName, not on ProductID, which violates 3NF. To make this 3NF compliant, you would create a separate table for suppliers:

Products Table:

ProductID	ProductName	SupplierName
101	Pen	OfficeGoods
102	Pencil	OfficeGoods

Suppliers Table:

SupplierName	SupplierCity
OfficeGoods	New York

HIGHER NORMAL FORMS

Beyond 3NF, there are other normal forms like **Boyce-Codd Normal Form (BCNF)**, **4NF**, and **5NF**, but they are used less frequently and apply to more specific cases. Generally, if your database is in 3NF, it is considered well-normalized for most applications.

BALANCING NORMALIZATION AND PERFORMANCE

While normalization brings many benefits, it's also important to strike a balance. Highly normalized databases can sometimes lead to performance issues due to the complexity of JOIN operations between multiple tables. For very high-read applications, **denormalization** (the opposite of normalization) may be used to improve performance, but this comes at the cost of data redundancy.

Example: A highly normalized database might store customer orders, products, and suppliers in separate tables, requiring multiple JOINs for a single query. In some cases, combining information into a single table may speed up reads but increase redundancy and storage use.

WHEN TO USE NORMALIZATION

1. **Data Consistency is Critical**: If maintaining consistency is crucial (e.g., banking, healthcare), stick to normalized designs to avoid data anomalies.
2. **Frequent Data Updates**: When the data is updated often, normalization can simplify updates, reducing errors.
3. **Storage is a Concern**: Normalization helps save storage by removing redundant data.

EXAMPLE OF A NORMALIZED DATABASE

Consider an e-commerce application with the following tables:

Customers:

CustomerID	Name	Email
1	John Doe	john@example.com
2	Jane Smith	jane@example.com

Orders:

OrderID	CustomerID	OrderDate
101	1	2024-01-15
102	2	2024-02-20

OrderDetails:

OrderDetailID	OrderID	ProductID	Quantity
1	101	201	3
2	102	202	5

Products:

ProductID	ProductName
201	Pen
202	Notebook

This design follows 3NF, with each table focusing on a specific entity, reducing redundancy and maintaining data integrity.

By understanding and applying normalization, you can design efficient, flexible, and robust databases.

BACKUP AND RESTORE

In any database management system, data loss can occur due to hardware failures, human errors, or even natural disasters. This is why having a robust backup and restore strategy is crucial. In MySQL, you can easily create backups of your databases and restore them when needed, ensuring that your data is safe and recoverable.

WHY BACKUP IS IMPORTANT

1. **Data Protection**: Regular backups protect your data from loss. If your database crashes or data becomes corrupted, you can restore it to a previous state.
2. **Disaster Recovery**: Backups allow you to recover from catastrophic events, such as server failures, power outages, or malicious attacks.
3. **Data Migration**: When upgrading or migrating databases, backups can help ensure a smooth transition without data loss.

BACKING UP YOUR DATABASE

MySQL provides several methods for backing up your databases:

1. Using mysqldump

The most common way to back up a MySQL database is by using the mysqldump command-line utility. This tool generates a .sql file containing all the SQL commands needed to recreate the database.

Example Command:

mysqldump -u username -p DatabaseName > backup.sql

- -u username: Specifies the MySQL user.
- -p: Prompts for the password.
- DatabaseName: The name of the database you want to back up.
- > backup.sql: Redirects the output to a file named backup.sql.

2. Backing Up All Databases

If you want to back up all databases on your MySQL server, you can use the --all-databases option:

mysqldump -u username -p --all-databases > all_databases_backup.sql

3. Using MySQL Workbench

If you prefer a graphical interface, you can also use MySQL Workbench to create backups. Here's how:

1. Open MySQL Workbench and connect to your database server.
2. Go to **Server** > **Data Export**.
3. Select the database you want to back up.
4. Choose the export options (e.g., export to a self-contained file).

5. Click **Start Export**.

4. Scheduled Backups

For automated backups, you can set up a cron job (on Linux) or a Task Scheduler (on Windows) to run the mysqldump command at specified intervals, ensuring that your data is backed up regularly without manual intervention.

RESTORING YOUR DATABASE

Restoring your database from a backup is just as important as creating one. MySQL allows you to restore a database from a .sql file created by mysqldump.

Restoring a Database

To restore a database from a backup, you can use the following command:

mysql -u username -p DatabaseName < backup.sql

- DatabaseName: The name of the database you want to restore.
- < backup.sql: Redirects the input from the backup file.

Restoring All Databases

If you backed up all databases, you can restore them with:

mysql -u username -p < all_databases_backup.sql

Important Considerations

1. **Ensure Database Exists**: Before restoring, ensure that the target database exists. If it doesn't, you can create it using the CREATE DATABASE statement.
2. **Overwriting Data**: Restoring a database will overwrite existing data. Be cautious and ensure you have the correct backup file.
3. **Data Consistency**: For large databases, ensure that your backup and restore processes maintain data consistency, especially if you have transactions occurring during the backup.

BACKUP STRATEGIES

To effectively protect your data, consider implementing a backup strategy that includes:

- **Full Backups**: Periodically back up the entire database. This is usually done weekly or monthly.
- **Incremental Backups**: Back up only the changes made since the last backup. This helps save time and storage space.
- **Off-Site Storage**: Store backups in a different physical location or use cloud storage to protect against local disasters.
- **Testing Restores**: Regularly test your backup and restore process to ensure that you can successfully recover your data when needed.

Backing up and restoring your MySQL database is a vital part of database administration. By understanding the backup methods available and creating a solid backup strategy, you can safeguard your data against loss and ensure quick recovery in case of emergencies. Next, we'll explore **User**

Management, where you'll learn how to control access to your MySQL databases.

USING EXPLAIN

Understanding how MySQL processes your queries is crucial for optimizing performance and ensuring efficient data retrieval. The EXPLAIN statement is a powerful tool that allows you to analyze and understand the execution plan of your SQL queries. By using EXPLAIN, you can identify potential bottlenecks, improve query performance, and make informed decisions about indexing and query structure.

WHAT IS EXPLAIN?

EXPLAIN provides information about how MySQL executes a query, detailing the steps taken and the resources used. When you prepend your query with EXPLAIN, MySQL returns a result set that includes important information such as:

- The order in which tables are accessed.
- The type of join used.
- The indexes that will be utilized.
- Estimated number of rows processed.
- The total cost of the query execution.

HOW TO USE EXPLAIN

To use EXPLAIN, simply add the keyword before your SQL statement. Here's an example:

EXPLAIN SELECT * FROM Employees WHERE department_id = 5;

Understanding the Output

When you execute an EXPLAIN statement, you will receive a result set with several columns. Here's what each of them means:

1. **id**: The identifier of the select, which helps in understanding the execution order of complex queries with subqueries.
2. **select_type**: Indicates the type of SELECT operation, such as SIMPLE (no subqueries), PRIMARY (the outermost SELECT), or SUBQUERY (a subquery).
3. **table**: The table being accessed.
4. **type**: The join type used, which ranges from the most efficient (e.g., const, eq_ref) to the least efficient (e.g., ALL).
5. **possible_keys**: Lists the indexes that could be used for the query.
6. **key**: The actual index used by MySQL to retrieve rows.
7. **key_len**: The length of the key used.
8. **ref**: Indicates which columns or constants are compared to the index.
9. **rows**: The estimated number of rows MySQL believes it will need to examine to execute the query.
10. **Extra**: Additional information about how MySQL resolves the query, including details like whether a temporary table is created or if a filesort is used.

INTERPRETING THE RESULTS

Here's an example output of an EXPLAIN statement:

id	select_type	table	type	possible_keys	key	key_len	ref	rows	Extra
1	SIMPLE	Employees	ref	idx_department_id	idx_department_id	4	const	10	Using where

- **Type**: The ref type indicates that MySQL will use an index to find the rows efficiently.
- **Possible Keys**: The presence of idx_department_id suggests that an index exists for department_id.
- **Rows**: The estimated value of 10 shows that MySQL anticipates scanning ten rows to satisfy the query.

OPTIMIZING QUERIES WITH EXPLAIN

1. **Identify Slow Queries**: Use EXPLAIN on queries that take a long time to execute to understand where the delays may occur.
2. **Optimize Joins**: Pay attention to the join types. If you see ALL, it indicates a full table scan, which may need optimization through indexing.
3. **Use Indexes Wisely**: Ensure that the correct indexes are being utilized. If possible_keys lists multiple indexes but key shows none, you may need to optimize your indexing strategy.
4. **Avoid Full Table Scans**: If possible, restructure your queries to use indexed columns to reduce the number of rows scanned.

LIMITATIONS OF EXPLAIN

While EXPLAIN is a powerful tool, keep in mind:

- The output may not reflect the exact performance in a live environment due to factors like caching and concurrent queries.

- Complex queries involving subqueries or multiple joins can result in more complicated execution plans that may require additional analysis.

Using EXPLAIN in MySQL is essential for understanding how your queries are executed and for identifying areas for optimization. By analyzing the output of EXPLAIN, you can make informed decisions about indexing and query structure, ultimately improving the performance of your database. In the next section, we will cover **Query Optimization Strategies**, where you will learn more about techniques to enhance query performance.

OPTIMIZING QUERIES

Optimizing queries in MySQL is crucial for ensuring that your database operates efficiently and delivers results quickly. As your data grows, poorly optimized queries can lead to slow response times, increased server load, and overall degraded performance. In this section, we will explore various strategies to optimize your queries, enhancing the speed and efficiency of your database interactions.

1. USE PROPER INDEXING

Indexes play a vital role in query performance. They allow MySQL to find rows quickly without scanning the entire table. Here are some best practices:

Identify Frequently Queried Columns: Analyze your queries to find which columns are often used in WHERE, JOIN, or ORDER BY clauses. Create indexes on these columns.

Use Composite Indexes: If your queries often filter or sort by multiple columns, consider creating composite indexes that include those columns.

Avoid Over-Indexing: While indexes speed up read operations, they can slow down write operations (INSERT, UPDATE, DELETE). Strike a balance by only indexing columns that will benefit from it.

2. AVOID SELECT *

Using SELECT * retrieves all columns from a table, which can lead to unnecessary data being transferred and processed. Instead, specify only the columns you need:

SELECT first_name, last_name FROM Employees WHERE department_id = 5;

This not only improves performance but also reduces the amount of data transmitted over the network.

3. USE LIMIT

When querying large datasets, using LIMIT can significantly improve performance by restricting the number of rows returned. This is particularly useful in applications where you only need a subset of the results:

```
SELECT * FROM Employees ORDER BY hire_date DESC LIMIT
10;
```

4. OPTIMIZE JOIN OPERATIONS

Joins can be resource-intensive, especially with large tables.
Here are tips for optimizing them:

Use INNER JOIN Instead of OUTER JOIN When Possible: If you
don't need all records from both tables, use INNER JOIN to
minimize data processed.

Filter Early: Apply filtering conditions as early as possible in
the query. This reduces the number of rows processed in
subsequent join operations.

Ensure Proper Indexing on Joined Columns: Make sure that
the columns used in join conditions are indexed to speed up
the join operation.

5. USE EXISTS OR IN Wisely

When checking for the existence of records in a subquery,
prefer EXISTS over IN if the subquery returns a large result set.
EXISTS stops searching as soon as it finds a matching row,
while IN evaluates all rows in the subquery:

```
-- Using EXISTS

SELECT * FROM Departments d

WHERE EXISTS (SELECT 1 FROM Employees e WHERE
e.department_id = d.id);
```

6. ANALYZE AND OPTIMIZE QUERIES WITH EXPLAIN

As discussed earlier, using the EXPLAIN statement helps you understand how MySQL executes your queries. Use it to identify slow parts of your queries and make adjustments based on the insights it provides.

7. AVOID FUNCTION CALLS ON INDEXED COLUMNS

Using functions on indexed columns in the WHERE clause can prevent MySQL from using the index. For example, avoid writing queries like this:

SELECT * FROM Employees WHERE YEAR(hire_date) = 2022;

Instead, rewrite the query to allow the index to be used:

SELECT * FROM Employees WHERE hire_date >= '2022-01-01' AND hire_date < '2023-01-01';

8. USE TEMPORARY TABLES

For complex queries involving multiple operations, consider breaking them down using temporary tables. This allows you to store intermediate results and simplify subsequent queries.

CREATE TEMPORARY TABLE TempResults AS

SELECT * FROM Employees WHERE department_id = 5;

SELECT * FROM TempResults WHERE hire_date > '2020-01-01';

9. REGULARLY ANALYZE AND OPTIMIZE YOUR DATABASE

Use MySQL's built-in tools like ANALYZE TABLE and OPTIMIZE TABLE to gather statistics and reorganize data for optimal performance.

ANALYZE TABLE Employees;

OPTIMIZE TABLE Employees;

By implementing these query optimization strategies, you can significantly enhance the performance of your MySQL database. Regularly monitor and analyze your queries, adapting your approach as your data and application needs evolve.

CONFIGURATION TUNING

Configuration tuning is essential for optimizing the performance of your MySQL database. MySQL comes with a variety of default settings that work well for general use cases, but as your application grows, these settings may need to be adjusted to better suit your specific workload and data size. In this section, we will discuss key configuration parameters and best practices to help you tune your MySQL server effectively.

1. UNDERSTANDING MY.CNF

The primary configuration file for MySQL is my.cnf (or my.ini on Windows). This file contains various settings that dictate how the MySQL server behaves. Common sections include:

- **[mysqld]**: Configuration options for the MySQL server.

- **[client]**: Settings for client programs, such as the MySQL command-line client.
- **[mysqld_safe]**: Options for the MySQL server's safe mode.

To locate my.cnf, check the default installation directory or run the command:

mysql --help | grep "Default options"

2. MEMORY ALLOCATION

a. INNODB_BUFFER_POOL_SIZE

The InnoDB buffer pool is a memory area where InnoDB caches data and indexes. Adjusting the innodb_buffer_pool_size setting can significantly impact performance. As a rule of thumb:

- Set this value to 70-80% of your server's total RAM for dedicated MySQL servers.

Example:

innodb_buffer_pool_size = 2G

b. QUERY_CACHE_SIZE

The query cache stores the results of SELECT statements, allowing MySQL to return cached results for identical queries without executing them again. However, with the introduction of InnoDB's row-level locking, excessive query cache use can lead to contention. Consider disabling it or setting a low size:

query_cache_type = 0

query_cache_size = 0

c. TEMP_BUFFER_SIZE

The tmp_table_size and max_heap_table_size settings control the maximum size of temporary tables. If your application uses temporary tables frequently, consider increasing these values:

tmp_table_size = 64M

max_heap_table_size = 64M

3. CONNECTION SETTINGS

a. MAX_CONNECTIONS

The max_connections setting determines how many simultaneous connections your MySQL server will allow. If you anticipate a high number of concurrent users, increase this value:

max_connections = 200

b. WAIT_TIMEOUT AND INTERACTIVE_TIMEOUT

These settings determine how long MySQL waits before closing idle connections. Adjusting them can help free up resources:

wait_timeout = 300

interactive_timeout = 300

4. I/O OPTIMIZATION

a. INNODB_FLUSH_METHOD

The innodb_flush_method setting controls how InnoDB flushes data to disk. For better performance, especially on SSDs, set this to O_DIRECT:

innodb_flush_method = O_DIRECT

b. INNODB_LOG_FILE_SIZE

The size of the InnoDB log file can impact performance, especially for write-heavy applications. Increase this size to reduce the frequency of log file flushing:

innodb_log_file_size = 512M

5. SLOW QUERY LOGGING

Enable the slow query log to identify and troubleshoot inefficient queries. This feature allows you to log queries that exceed a specified execution time:

slow_query_log = 1

slow_query_log_file = /var/log/mysql/slow-query.log

long_query_time = 2

6. MONITORING AND ADJUSTING

After making configuration changes, it's important to monitor the performance of your MySQL server. Use tools like MySQL Workbench, performance_schema, or third-party monitoring solutions to analyze query performance, resource usage, and system health.

a. PERFORMANCE_SCHEMA

Enable the performance_schema to gather detailed metrics about your server's performance:

performance_schema = ON

7. REGULARLY BACKUP YOUR CONFIGURATION

Before making significant changes, back up your existing my.cnf file. This ensures you can revert to a stable configuration if needed.

cp /etc/my.cnf /etc/my.cnf.bak

Configuration tuning is an ongoing process that requires regular assessment and adjustment as your application evolves.

By understanding and optimizing key MySQL settings, you can significantly improve the performance and reliability of your database.

USING GROUP_CONCAT

The GROUP_CONCAT function is a powerful aggregate function in MySQL that allows you to concatenate values from multiple rows into a single string. This can be particularly useful for generating lists or summaries from grouped data. In this section, we will explore how to use GROUP_CONCAT, its syntax, and practical examples.

1. SYNTAX

The basic syntax of the GROUP_CONCAT function is as follows:

GROUP_CONCAT(expression [ORDER BY expression] [SEPARATOR 'separator'])

- **expression**: The column or expression to concatenate.
- **ORDER BY**: Optional. Specifies the order of the concatenated values.
- **SEPARATOR**: Optional. Specifies a string to separate the concatenated values (default is a comma).

2. EXAMPLE SCENARIO

Let's say we have a students table with the following structure:

CREATE TABLE students (

  id INT PRIMARY KEY,

  name VARCHAR(100),

  class VARCHAR(10)

);

And the following data:

id	name	class
1	Alice	10A
2	Bob	10A
3	Charlie	10B
4	David	10B
5	Eve	10A

3. CONCATENATING NAMES BY CLASS

If we want to create a list of student names grouped by their class, we can use GROUP_CONCAT like this:

SELECT class, GROUP_CONCAT(name ORDER BY name SEPARATOR ', ') AS student_names

FROM students

GROUP BY class;

Result:

class	student_names
10A	Alice, Bob, Eve
10B	Charlie, David

4. CUSTOM SEPARATOR

You can customize the separator to fit your needs. For instance, if you want to separate names with a semicolon, you can modify the query as follows:

```
SELECT class, GROUP_CONCAT(name ORDER BY name
SEPARATOR '; ') AS student_names

FROM students

GROUP BY class;
```

Result:

class student_names
10A   Alice; Bob; Eve
10B   Charlie; David

5. HANDLING NULL VALUES

When using GROUP_CONCAT, any NULL values in the concatenated expression will be ignored. For example, if one of the students had a NULL name, it would not appear in the result.

6. LIMITING RESULTS

You can limit the number of values concatenated by using the LIMIT clause in the GROUP_CONCAT function. For instance, if you only want to show the first two names in each class:

```
SELECT class, GROUP_CONCAT(name ORDER BY name
SEPARATOR ', ' LIMIT 2) AS student_names

FROM students

GROUP BY class;
```

Result:

class	student_names
10A	Alice, Bob
10B	Charlie, David

The GROUP_CONCAT function is a versatile tool for aggregating and presenting data in a concise format. By understanding how to use this function effectively, you can enhance your ability to generate meaningful reports and summaries from your MySQL databases.

JSON DATA TYPE

MySQL supports a native **JSON** data type, which allows you to store and manipulate JSON (JavaScript Object Notation) formatted data directly in your database. This feature is especially useful for applications that require flexible data structures or need to handle semi-structured data.

1. INTRODUCTION TO JSON

JSON is a lightweight data interchange format that is easy for humans to read and write and easy for machines to parse and generate. It represents data as key-value pairs, arrays, and nested objects, making it a popular choice for web applications and APIs.

Example of JSON Format

```json
{
    "name": "Alice",
    "age": 30,
    "is_student": false,
    "courses": ["Math", "Science"],
    "address": {
        "street": "123 Main St",
        "city": "Anytown"
    }
}
```

2. CREATING A TABLE WITH JSON

To use the JSON data type in MySQL, you can create a table with a JSON column. Here's how you can create a users table that includes a JSON column:

```sql
CREATE TABLE users (
    id INT AUTO_INCREMENT PRIMARY KEY,
    name VARCHAR(100),
    details JSON
```

);

3. INSERTING JSON DATA

You can insert JSON data into the table like this:

INSERT INTO users (name, details) VALUES ('Alice', '{"age": 30, "is_student": false, "courses": ["Math", "Science"], "address": {"street": "123 Main St", "city": "Anytown"}}');

Important Notes:

- Ensure that the JSON data is valid. MySQL will reject invalid JSON formats.
- You can also use prepared statements in your application code to insert JSON data safely.

4. QUERYING JSON DATA

MySQL provides several functions to query and manipulate JSON data. Here are a few examples:

4.1 Accessing JSON Values

To extract specific values from the JSON data, you can use the -> operator or the JSON_EXTRACT function.

Example:

SELECT name, details->'$.age' AS age

FROM users;

4.2 Filtering Based on JSON Values

You can filter results based on values within the JSON column using the JSON_UNQUOTE and JSON_EXTRACT functions.

Example:

SELECT name

FROM users

WHERE JSON_UNQUOTE(details->'$.is_student') = 'false';

4.3 Modifying JSON Data

You can modify existing JSON data using the JSON_SET, JSON_REPLACE, and JSON_REMOVE functions.

Example:

UPDATE users

SET details = JSON_SET(details, '$.age', 31)

WHERE name = 'Alice';

4.4 Adding New JSON Keys

You can add new key-value pairs to the JSON data as follows:

UPDATE users

SET details = JSON_SET(details, '$.email', 'alice@example.com')

WHERE name = 'Alice';

5. INDEXING JSON DATA

To improve query performance, you can create indexes on JSON values. MySQL allows you to create a generated column based on a JSON value and index that column.

Example:

ALTER TABLE users

ADD COLUMN age INT GENERATED ALWAYS AS (JSON_UNQUOTE(details->'$.age')) STORED,

ADD INDEX idx_age (age);

The JSON data type in MySQL provides a flexible way to store and manage semi-structured data. By understanding how to work with JSON in MySQL, you can take advantage of its capabilities to handle diverse data structures in your applications.

FULL-TEXT SEARCH

Full-Text Search in MySQL allows you to perform complex searches on textual data, enabling you to find words or phrases within large text fields efficiently. This feature is especially useful for applications that involve searching documents, articles, or any text-heavy data.

1. INTRODUCTION TO FULL-TEXT SEARCH

MySQL provides a full-text search capability for columns of type CHAR, VARCHAR, or TEXT. Unlike standard string comparison operators, full-text searches can handle natural language queries and are optimized for speed and relevance.

Key Features:

- Support for natural language queries.
- Ranking of results based on relevance.
- Support for boolean search modes.

2. ENABLING FULL-TEXT SEARCH

To use full-text search, you need to create a full-text index on the columns you wish to search. Here's how to do it:

Example: Creating a Table with a Full-Text Index

```
CREATE TABLE articles (

    id INT AUTO_INCREMENT PRIMARY KEY,

    title VARCHAR(255),

    body TEXT,

    FULLTEXT(title, body)

);
```

3. INSERTING DATA

You can insert data into the articles table as follows:

```
INSERT INTO articles (title, body)

VALUES

('MySQL Tutorial', 'Learn how to use MySQL with practical
examples.'),

('Full-Text Search in MySQL', 'This article explains full-text
search capabilities in MySQL.');
```

4. PERFORMING FULL-TEXT SEARCHES

Once you have your data and index set up, you can perform
full-text searches using the MATCH() and AGAINST() functions.

4.1 Basic Full-Text Search

To search for articles containing specific words, you can use
the following syntax:

```
SELECT *

FROM articles

WHERE MATCH(title, body) AGAINST('MySQL');
```

4.2 Natural Language Mode

In natural language mode, MySQL interprets the search string
as a natural language query, returning relevant results:

```
SELECT *
```

FROM articles

WHERE MATCH(title, body) AGAINST('search capabilities');

4.3 Boolean Mode

Boolean mode allows for more advanced searching techniques, such as including or excluding specific terms. You can use symbols like + (must include) and - (must not include).

```
SELECT *

FROM articles

WHERE MATCH(title, body) AGAINST('+MySQL -Tutorial' IN
BOOLEAN MODE);
```

5. RANKING SEARCH RESULTS

The results of a full-text search are ranked based on their relevance to the search query. You can retrieve the relevance score by using the MATCH() function along with AGAINST().

Example: Retrieving Results with Relevance Scores

```
SELECT *, MATCH(title, body) AGAINST('MySQL') AS relevance

FROM articles

WHERE MATCH(title, body) AGAINST('MySQL')

ORDER BY relevance DESC;
```

6. LIMITING SEARCH RESULTS

To limit the number of results returned by your search query, you can use the LIMIT clause:

SELECT *

FROM articles

WHERE MATCH(title, body) AGAINST('MySQL')

LIMIT 5;

Full-Text Search in MySQL is a powerful feature for efficiently querying textual data. By leveraging full-text indexes and search capabilities, you can enhance the search functionality of your applications

SUBQUERIES

Subqueries, or nested queries, are a powerful feature in MySQL that allows you to use the result of one query as an input for another query. This capability can simplify complex SQL operations and enhance data retrieval.

1. WHAT IS A SUBQUERY?

A subquery is a SQL query embedded within another query. It can return a single value, a list of values, or a table. Subqueries can be used in various clauses, such as SELECT, FROM, WHERE, and HAVING.

Key Features:

- Enables complex queries to be broken down into simpler parts.
- Can improve the readability of your SQL statements.
- Helps in filtering results based on the output of another query.

2. TYPES OF SUBQUERIES

There are two main types of subqueries:

2.1 Single-Value Subqueries

These subqueries return a single value and can be used in a comparison operation.

Example: Using a Single-Value Subquery

SELECT name, salary

FROM employees

WHERE salary > (SELECT AVG(salary) FROM employees);

In this example, the subquery calculates the average salary of all employees, and the main query retrieves the names and salaries of employees earning above that average.

2.2 Multi-Value Subqueries

These subqueries return multiple values and are typically used with the IN operator or in a JOIN.

Example: Using a Multi-Value Subquery

SELECT name

FROM employees

WHERE department_id IN (SELECT id FROM departments WHERE location = 'New York');

Here, the subquery retrieves all department IDs located in New York, and the main query selects employees from those departments.

3. SUBQUERIES IN SELECT CLAUSES

You can also use subqueries in the SELECT clause to compute additional columns.

Example: Adding a Subquery in the SELECT Clause

SELECT name,

   (SELECT COUNT(*) FROM projects WHERE employee_id = employees.id) AS project_count

FROM employees;

In this example, the subquery counts the number of projects for each employee, providing a count alongside their name.

4. SUBQUERIES IN FROM CLAUSES

Subqueries can be used in the FROM clause to create a temporary table.

Example: Using a Subquery in the FROM Clause

SELECT department_name, avg_salary

FROM (SELECT department_id, AVG(salary) AS avg_salary

   FROM employees

   GROUP BY department_id) AS dept_avg

JOIN departments ON dept_avg.department_id = departments.id;

In this case, the subquery calculates the average salary for each department, and the main query joins this result with the departments table to retrieve department names.

5. PERFORMANCE CONSIDERATIONS

While subqueries are useful, they can sometimes lead to performance issues, especially if not optimized properly. Consider the following tips:

- Use joins instead of subqueries when possible, as they are often more efficient.
- Ensure that the subquery returns a reasonable number of rows to prevent excessive processing.
- Always test and analyze the performance of your queries, especially when dealing with large datasets.

Subqueries are a valuable tool in MySQL that allow you to perform complex data retrieval operations with ease. By understanding how to effectively use subqueries, you can write more powerful and efficient SQL queries.

TEMPORARY TABLES

Temporary tables in MySQL are a useful feature that allows you to store and manipulate data for the duration of a session or until they are explicitly dropped. They are particularly beneficial when working with complex queries that require intermediate results without affecting the main database schema.

1. WHAT ARE TEMPORARY TABLES?

Temporary tables are special tables that exist temporarily during a session. They are created in the TEMPORARY table space and are automatically dropped when the session ends or the table is explicitly deleted. Unlike regular tables, temporary tables are isolated, meaning that they are not visible to other sessions.

Key Features:

- **Session-Specific:** Each session can create its own temporary tables without interfering with others.
- **Automatic Cleanup:** Temporary tables are dropped automatically when the session ends, ensuring no leftover data.
- **Performance:** They can enhance performance by storing intermediate results and reducing the complexity of complex queries.

160

2. CREATING TEMPORARY TABLES

To create a temporary table, you use the CREATE TEMPORARY TABLE statement, similar to creating a regular table.

Example: Creating a Temporary Table

CREATE TEMPORARY TABLE temp_sales (

  product_id INT,

  quantity_sold INT,

  sale_date DATE

);

In this example, we create a temporary table named temp_sales with three columns: product_id, quantity_sold, and sale_date.

3. INSERTING DATA INTO TEMPORARY TABLES

You can insert data into temporary tables using the INSERT statement, just as you would with regular tables.

Example: Inserting Data

INSERT INTO temp_sales (product_id, quantity_sold, sale_date)

VALUES (1, 100, '2024-10-01'),

  (2, 150, '2024-10-02'),

(3, 200, '2024-10-03');

This example inserts three rows of sales data into the temp_sales table.

4. QUERYING TEMPORARY TABLES

You can query temporary tables just like any other table. The data is accessible only within the session that created the table.

Example: Querying Data

SELECT * FROM temp_sales;

This statement retrieves all rows from the temp_sales table.

5. USING TEMPORARY TABLES FOR COMPLEX QUERIES

Temporary tables are especially useful when you need to perform multiple operations on a set of data. For instance, you might want to aggregate data before joining it with other tables.

Example: Using a Temporary Table in a Complex Query

CREATE TEMPORARY TABLE temp_summary AS

SELECT product_id, SUM(quantity_sold) AS total_quantity

FROM temp_sales

GROUP BY product_id;

SELECT d.product_name, ts.total_quantity

FROM temp_summary ts

JOIN products d ON ts.product_id = d.id;

In this example, we first create a temporary table called temp_summary that stores the total quantity sold for each product. Then, we join this temporary table with the products table to retrieve product names alongside their total quantities sold.

6. DROPPING TEMPORARY TABLES

While temporary tables are automatically dropped at the end of a session, you can also drop them manually using the DROP statement.

Example: Dropping a Temporary Table

DROP TEMPORARY TABLE IF EXISTS temp_sales;

This statement checks if the temp_sales table exists and drops it if it does.

Temporary tables are an invaluable feature in MySQL that facilitate complex data manipulation without the risks associated with permanent changes to the database schema. By effectively utilizing temporary tables, you can streamline your queries and improve performance.

STORED FUNCTIONS

Stored functions in MySQL are routines that allow you to encapsulate reusable logic within the database. Unlike stored procedures, which may perform actions but do not return a value, stored functions always return a single value and can be used within SQL expressions, making them incredibly versatile for complex calculations and data manipulation.

1. WHAT ARE STORED FUNCTIONS?

Stored functions are similar to functions in programming languages. They are defined once and can be executed multiple times, which helps in reducing code duplication and improving maintainability. You can use stored functions to perform calculations, manipulate data, or return a value based on input parameters.

Key Features:

- **Reusable Logic:** Define complex logic once and reuse it in multiple queries.
- **Return Values:** Always return a single value, which can be used in SQL expressions.
- **Encapsulation:** Encapsulate logic within the database for improved organization.

2. CREATING A STORED FUNCTION

To create a stored function, you use the CREATE FUNCTION statement. This includes specifying the function name, input parameters, return type, and the function body.

Example: Creating a Stored Function

DELIMITER //

CREATE FUNCTION calculate_discount(price DECIMAL(10, 2), discount_rate DECIMAL(5, 2))

RETURNS DECIMAL(10, 2)

BEGIN

   DECLARE discount_amount DECIMAL(10, 2);

   SET discount_amount = price * discount_rate / 100;

   RETURN price - discount_amount;

END //

DELIMITER ;

In this example, we create a stored function named calculate_discount that takes two parameters: price and discount_rate. It calculates the discount amount and returns the final price after applying the discount.

3. USING STORED FUNCTIONS

Once a stored function is created, you can use it just like a built-in MySQL function. You can call the function in your SQL queries, passing the required arguments.

Example: Calling a Stored Function

SELECT   product_id,   calculate_discount(price,   10)   AS discounted_price

FROM products;

This query retrieves the product_id and the discounted price for each product by calling the calculate_discount function with a discount rate of 10%.

4. UPDATING AND DROPPING STORED FUNCTIONS

You can modify a stored function using the DROP statement followed by the creation of a new function with the same name. To remove a stored function, use the DROP FUNCTION statement.

Example: Dropping a Stored Function

DROP FUNCTION IF EXISTS calculate_discount;

This statement checks if the calculate_discount function exists and drops it if it does.

5. ERROR HANDLING IN STORED FUNCTIONS

MySQL allows you to handle errors within stored functions using condition handlers. This provides a way to manage exceptions that may occur during execution.

Example: Error Handling

DELIMITER //

CREATE FUNCTION safe_divide(numerator DECIMAL(10, 2), denominator DECIMAL(10, 2))

RETURNS DECIMAL(10, 2)

BEGIN

  DECLARE result DECIMAL(10, 2);

  DECLARE CONTINUE HANDLER FOR SQLEXCEPTION SET result = NULL;

  IF denominator = 0 THEN

    RETURN NULL; -- Avoid division by zero

  END IF;

  SET result = numerator / denominator;

```
RETURN result;

END //
```

```
DELIMITER ;
```

In this example, the safe_divide function handles division by zero by returning NULL. The CONTINUE HANDLER ensures that the function does not terminate unexpectedly.

Stored functions are a powerful feature in MySQL that enable you to encapsulate and reuse complex logic within your database. By utilizing stored functions, you can simplify your SQL queries, improve maintainability, and ensure consistency across your data operations.

ERROR HANDLING

Error handling is a crucial aspect of programming and database management, allowing you to manage and respond to errors gracefully. In MySQL, proper error handling can help you prevent unexpected termination of operations and maintain the integrity of your database.

1. UNDERSTANDING ERRORS IN MYSQL

Errors in MySQL can occur for various reasons, such as syntax mistakes, data type mismatches, constraint violations, or issues with the underlying data. When an error occurs, MySQL typically raises an error message that indicates the nature of the problem.

Common Types of Errors:

- **Syntax Errors:** Occur due to incorrect SQL syntax.
- **Data Type Errors:** Arise when data types do not match.
- **Constraint Violations:** Happen when operations violate database constraints (e.g., primary key, foreign key).
- **Division by Zero:** Occurs when you attempt to divide a number by zero.

2. USING DECLARE HANDLER

MySQL provides a way to handle errors using the DECLARE HANDLER statement. This allows you to define actions that occur when specific conditions are met, such as encountering an error or warning.

Example: Basic Error Handling with CONTINUE HANDLER

```
DELIMITER //


CREATE PROCEDURE example_procedure()

BEGIN

  DECLARE EXIT HANDLER FOR SQLEXCEPTION

  BEGIN

    -- Error handling logic

    SELECT 'An error occurred!';
```

END;


```
-- A sample SQL operation that may cause an error

INSERT INTO products (product_name, price) VALUES
('Sample Product', -10);

END //
```


```
DELIMITER ;
```

In this example, if the INSERT statement fails (e.g., due to a negative price), the EXIT HANDLER executes the logic defined within it, providing an error message.

3. ERROR CODE AND MESSAGE

You can also retrieve specific error codes and messages to gain insights into the nature of the error. This can be helpful for debugging and logging purposes.

Example: Retrieving Error Information

```
DELIMITER //


CREATE PROCEDURE get_error_info()
```

```
BEGIN

    DECLARE error_message VARCHAR(255);

    DECLARE error_code INT;


    -- Sample operation

    INSERT INTO products (product_name, price) VALUES ('Test
Product', 'not_a_number');


    -- Handle any SQL exceptions

    DECLARE CONTINUE HANDLER FOR SQLEXCEPTION

    BEGIN

        -- Get the error code and message

        GET DIAGNOSTICS CONDITION 1

            error_code = RETURNED_SQLSTATE,

            error_message = MESSAGE_TEXT;


        SELECT CONCAT('Error Code: ', error_code, ', Message: ',
error_message) AS error_info;
```

```
  END;

END //
```

```
DELIMITER ;
```

In this example, if the INSERT operation fails, the error code and message are retrieved and displayed.

4. TRANSACTIONS AND ERROR HANDLING

Using transactions in combination with error handling allows you to ensure that your database remains consistent. If an error occurs during a transaction, you can roll back the entire transaction to its previous state.

Example: Using Transactions with Error Handling

```
DELIMITER //

CREATE PROCEDURE transaction_example()

BEGIN

  DECLARE EXIT HANDLER FOR SQLEXCEPTION

  BEGIN

    ROLLBACK; -- Rollback the transaction on error
```

```
    SELECT 'Transaction rolled back due to an error.';

END;


    START TRANSACTION;


    -- Sample operations

    INSERT INTO products (product_name, price) VALUES
('Product A', 100);

    INSERT INTO products (product_name, price) VALUES
('Product B', -50); -- This will cause an error


    COMMIT; -- Commit the transaction if no errors occurred

END //


DELIMITER ;
```

In this example, if any of the operations within the transaction fail, the entire transaction is rolled back, ensuring data integrity.

Error handling in MySQL is essential for creating robust and reliable database applications. By using DECLARE HANDLER statements and transactions effectively, you can manage errors gracefully, maintain data integrity, and provide clear feedback in case of issues.

USE CASE

The CASE statement in MySQL is a powerful conditional expression that allows you to perform different actions based on specific conditions. It can be used in various contexts, such as in SELECT queries, UPDATE statements, and ORDER BY clauses. The CASE statement provides a way to implement conditional logic directly within your SQL queries.

1. SYNTAX OF CASE

The CASE statement has two forms: **simple case** and **searched case**.

Simple CASE

In the simple case, you compare a single expression against a set of possible values.

CASE expression

  WHEN value1 THEN result1

  WHEN value2 THEN result2

...

ELSE resultN

END

Searched CASE

In the searched case, you evaluate multiple Boolean expressions.

CASE

WHEN condition1 THEN result1

WHEN condition2 THEN result2

...

ELSE resultN

END

2. USING CASE IN SELECT STATEMENTS

One of the most common uses of the CASE statement is within SELECT statements to categorize or transform data based on specific conditions.

Example: Categorizing Sales Data

Let's say you have a table named sales that contains information about sales transactions, including the amount.

You want to categorize each transaction as "Low," "Medium," or "High" based on the sale amount.

SELECT

  transaction_id,

  amount,

  CASE

    WHEN amount < 100 THEN 'Low'

    WHEN amount BETWEEN 100 AND 500 THEN 'Medium'

    ELSE 'High'

  END AS category

FROM sales;

In this example, the CASE statement categorizes each transaction based on the amount, resulting in a new column called category.

3. USING CASE IN ORDER BY CLAUSE

You can also use the CASE statement in the ORDER BY clause to customize the sort order based on specific conditions.

Example: Custom Sorting

Suppose you want to sort a list of products based on their stock status. If a product is in stock, you want it to appear first, followed by out-of-stock products.

SELECT

    product_name,

    stock_quantity

FROM products

ORDER BY

    CASE

      WHEN stock_quantity > 0 THEN 0 -- In stock

      ELSE 1 -- Out of stock

    END,

    product_name; -- Secondary sort by product name

In this example, products that are in stock appear first, followed by those that are out of stock, with a secondary sort by product_name.

4. USING CASE IN UPDATE STATEMENTS

You can also use the CASE statement in UPDATE statements to conditionally update values in a table.

Example: Updating Status

Assume you have a users table and you want to update the status column based on the last_login date.

UPDATE users

SET status = CASE

   WHEN last_login > NOW() - INTERVAL 30 DAY THEN 'Active'

   WHEN last_login BETWEEN NOW() - INTERVAL 30 DAY AND NOW() - INTERVAL 90 DAY THEN 'Inactive'

   ELSE 'Archived'

END;

In this example, the status of each user is updated based on how recently they logged in.

5. NESTING CASE STATEMENTS

You can also nest CASE statements to handle more complex conditions.

Example: Nested CASE

SELECT

   product_name,

   stock_quantity,

```
CASE

    WHEN stock_quantity > 100 THEN 'In Abundance'

    WHEN stock_quantity > 0 THEN

        CASE

            WHEN stock_quantity < 10 THEN 'Low Stock'

            ELSE 'Sufficient Stock'

        END

    ELSE 'Out of Stock'

    END AS stock_status

FROM products;
```

In this example, the outer CASE evaluates the stock quantity, and the inner CASE provides additional categorization for products with low stock.

The CASE statement in MySQL is a versatile tool for implementing conditional logic within your SQL queries. Whether you are categorizing data in a SELECT statement, customizing sort order in an ORDER BY clause, or conditionally updating records in an UPDATE statement, the CASE statement can enhance your data manipulation capabilities.

PARTITIONING

Partitioning is a powerful feature in MySQL that allows you to divide a large table into smaller, more manageable pieces, while still treating them as a single table. This can enhance performance, improve manageability, and simplify data maintenance tasks. In this section, we'll explore what partitioning is, its benefits, the types of partitioning available in MySQL, and how to implement it.

1. WHAT IS PARTITIONING?

When you partition a table, you are effectively splitting it into smaller, more manageable segments called partitions. Each partition can store a subset of the table's data, allowing for more efficient data retrieval and maintenance. The partitions can be based on various criteria, such as ranges of values or lists of values.

2. BENEFITS OF PARTITIONING

Partitioning offers several advantages:

- **Improved Performance**: By accessing only the relevant partitions, queries can execute faster, especially on large datasets.
- **Easier Maintenance**: You can manage partitions individually. For example, you can drop or archive old partitions without affecting the entire table.
- **Enhanced Data Management**: Partitioning can help with data retention policies by allowing you to easily separate older data from newer data.

3. TYPES OF PARTITIONING IN MYSQL

MySQL supports several partitioning types:

3.1 Range Partitioning

In range partitioning, data is distributed across partitions based on a specified range of values in a column. This is useful for data that is chronologically ordered, like dates.

Example:

```
CREATE TABLE orders (

    order_id INT,

    order_date DATE,

    amount DECIMAL(10, 2)

) PARTITION BY RANGE (YEAR(order_date)) (

    PARTITION p0 VALUES LESS THAN (2021),

    PARTITION p1 VALUES LESS THAN (2022),

    PARTITION p2 VALUES LESS THAN (2023)

);
```

3.2 List Partitioning

List partitioning distributes data across partitions based on a set of discrete values. This is useful for categorical data.

Example:

CREATE TABLE employees (

   emp_id INT,

   department VARCHAR(50)

) PARTITION BY LIST (department) (

   PARTITION p_sales VALUES IN ('Sales'),

   PARTITION p_hr VALUES IN ('HR'),

   PARTITION p_it VALUES IN ('IT')

);

3.3 Hash Partitioning

Hash partitioning distributes data evenly across a specified number of partitions based on a hashing algorithm applied to a specified column. This is useful for load balancing.

Example:

CREATE TABLE customers (

   customer_id INT,

name VARCHAR(100)

) PARTITION BY HASH (customer_id) PARTITIONS 4;

3.4 Key Partitioning

Key partitioning is similar to hash partitioning but uses a MySQL-provided partitioning function that allows for more efficient distribution of data across partitions.

Example:

CREATE TABLE products (

   product_id INT,

   category VARCHAR(50)

) PARTITION BY KEY (product_id) PARTITIONS 4;

CREATE TABLE products (

   product_id INT,

   category VARCHAR(50)

) PARTITION BY KEY (product_id) PARTITIONS 4;

4. CREATING PARTITIONED TABLES

When creating a partitioned table, you specify the partitioning scheme in the CREATE TABLE statement.

Example: Creating a Partitioned Table

```
CREATE TABLE transactions (

    transaction_id INT,

    transaction_date DATE,

    amount DECIMAL(10, 2)

) PARTITION BY RANGE (MONTH(transaction_date)) (

    PARTITION jan VALUES LESS THAN (2),

    PARTITION feb VALUES LESS THAN (3),

    PARTITION mar VALUES LESS THAN (4)

);
```

5. MANAGING PARTITIONS

Once you have partitioned a table, you can perform various operations to manage the partitions.

5.1 Adding a Partition

You can add a new partition using the ALTER TABLE statement:

```
ALTER TABLE transactions ADD PARTITION (

    PARTITION apr VALUES LESS THAN (5)
```

);

5.2 Dropping a Partition

You can remove a partition if it is no longer needed:

ALTER TABLE transactions DROP PARTITION jan;

5.3 Merging Partitions

You can merge two or more partitions into one:

ALTER TABLE transactions COALESCE PARTITION 2;

Partitioning is a powerful tool in MySQL that can significantly enhance performance and manageability for large datasets. By understanding the different types of partitioning and how to implement them, you can optimize your database structure for better efficiency.

INDEX MAINTENANCE

Indexes play a crucial role in optimizing query performance in MySQL by allowing the database to find rows more quickly. However, maintaining these indexes is equally important to ensure they remain efficient and effective. In this section, we will explore the significance of index maintenance, best practices for maintaining indexes, and techniques for monitoring and optimizing their performance.

1. WHAT IS INDEX MAINTENANCE?

Index maintenance refers to the processes involved in managing and optimizing indexes in a database. This includes ensuring that indexes are up to date, rebuilding or reorganizing them when necessary, and monitoring their impact on overall database performance.

2. IMPORTANCE OF INDEX MAINTENANCE

Proper index maintenance helps to:

- **Improve Query Performance**: Well-maintained indexes can significantly speed up data retrieval, leading to faster query execution.
- **Optimize Storage**: Regular maintenance can reduce the size of indexes, freeing up storage space.
- **Enhance Write Performance**: Keeping indexes updated can minimize the overhead associated with insert, update, and delete operations.

3. BEST PRACTICES FOR INDEX MAINTENANCE

3.1 Regularly Monitor Index Usage

To maintain optimal index performance, regularly monitor how indexes are being used. Use the SHOW INDEX command to gather information about index statistics:

SHOW INDEX FROM table_name;

This command provides valuable insights into index usage, including the number of times an index has been used and whether it is effective for the queries being executed.

3.2 Analyze and Optimize Indexes

Utilize the ANALYZE TABLE statement to gather statistics about table contents and help the query optimizer make informed decisions:

ANALYZE TABLE table_name;

After analyzing, consider running the OPTIMIZE TABLE statement to reorganize and defragment the table and its indexes:

OPTIMIZE TABLE table_name;

3.3 Remove Unused Indexes

Over time, some indexes may become unnecessary due to changes in application logic or query patterns. Regularly review your indexes and drop those that are no longer used to improve performance and reduce storage:

DROP INDEX index_name ON table_name;

3.4 Rebuild Fragmented Indexes

Indexes can become fragmented over time, especially with frequent insert, update, and delete operations. Rebuilding fragmented indexes can improve performance. In MySQL, you can rebuild an index by dropping and recreating it or using the ALTER TABLE statement:

ALTER TABLE table_name DROP INDEX index_name, ADD INDEX index_name (column1, column2);

4. MONITORING INDEX PERFORMANCE

Monitoring tools can help you identify performance issues related to indexes. Use the following techniques to keep an eye on index performance:

4.1 Query Execution Plans

Use the EXPLAIN statement to analyze how MySQL executes queries and to check whether the expected indexes are being utilized:

EXPLAIN SELECT * FROM table_name WHERE column_name = value;

This will provide a breakdown of how the query is executed and the indexes used, helping you determine if any indexes need attention.

4.2 Performance Schema

MySQL's Performance Schema can be enabled to track index usage and performance metrics. This feature provides a wealth of information for diagnosing performance issues.

4.3 Slow Query Log

Enable the slow query log to capture queries that take longer than a specified duration. This log can highlight queries that may benefit from better indexing.

SET GLOBAL slow_query_log = 'ON';

SET GLOBAL long_query_time = 1; -- time in seconds

Effective index maintenance is essential for optimizing the performance of your MySQL databases. By regularly monitoring index usage, analyzing and optimizing indexes, and rebuilding fragmented indexes, you can ensure your database remains efficient and responsive.

REPLICATION

Replication is a powerful feature in MySQL that allows you to create copies of your database across multiple servers. This capability is vital for enhancing data availability, improving read performance, and providing backup solutions. In this section, we will explore the different types of replication available in MySQL, how to set it up, and best practices for managing replication.

1. WHAT IS REPLICATION?

Replication is the process of copying data from one MySQL server (the master) to one or more other servers (the slaves). This ensures that the data remains consistent across different servers, enabling you to distribute the workload, increase redundancy, and provide fault tolerance.

2. TYPES OF REPLICATION

MySQL supports several types of replication, each with its own use cases:

2.1 Asynchronous Replication

In asynchronous replication, the master server sends updates to the slave servers, but it does not wait for confirmation that the changes have been applied. This is the most common type of replication and is suitable for scenarios where some delay in data consistency is acceptable.

2.2 Semi-Synchronous Replication

Semi-synchronous replication strikes a balance between asynchronous and synchronous replication. In this mode, the master server waits for at least one slave to acknowledge that it has received the data before proceeding. This ensures a higher level of data consistency while still allowing for improved performance compared to full synchronous replication.

2.3 Synchronous Replication

In synchronous replication, the master server waits for all slave servers to confirm that they have applied the changes before it commits the transaction. While this guarantees data consistency, it can introduce significant latency and is typically used in high-availability scenarios.

3. SETTING UP REPLICATION

3.1 Prepare the Master Server

Configure the Master Server: Edit the MySQL configuration file (my.cnf or my.ini) on the master server to enable binary logging, which is necessary for replication:

190

[mysqld]

log-bin=mysql-bin

server-id=1

log-bin: Enables binary logging, which is essential for replication.

server-id: A unique identifier for the master server.

Restart MySQL: Restart the MySQL service to apply the changes.

Create a Replication User: Create a dedicated user for replication purposes:

CREATE USER 'replicator'@'%' IDENTIFIED BY 'password';

GRANT REPLICATION SLAVE ON *.* TO 'replicator'@'%';

Prepare the Slave Server

Configure the Slave Server: On the slave server, configure it similarly in the MySQL configuration file:

[mysqld]

server-id=2

Restart MySQL: Restart the MySQL service to apply the changes.

Start Replication: Use the CHANGE MASTER TO command to configure the slave server to connect to the master server:

```
CHANGE MASTER TO

  MASTER_HOST='master_ip',

  MASTER_USER='replicator',

  MASTER_PASSWORD='password',

  MASTER_LOG_FILE='mysql-bin.000001',

  MASTER_LOG_POS=0;
```

Replace master_ip with the IP address of the master server.

The MASTER_LOG_FILE and MASTER_LOG_POS values should correspond to the binary log file and position from which the slave should start replicating.

Start the Slave: Finally, start the slave thread:

```
START SLAVE;
```

Monitor Replication

You can monitor the status of replication using the following command on the slave server:

```
SHOW SLAVE STATUS\G;
```

This command provides detailed information about the replication process, including whether the slave is running and any errors encountered.

4. BEST PRACTICES FOR REPLICATION

Use Unique Server IDs: Ensure that each server in your replication setup has a unique server-id to avoid conflicts.

Regularly Monitor Replication Status: Use monitoring tools to keep an eye on replication lag and other metrics.

Implement Backups: Even with replication in place, it's essential to perform regular backups to safeguard against data loss.

Test Failover Procedures: Regularly test your failover and recovery procedures to ensure they work as expected in a real-world scenario.

Replication is a critical component of MySQL that enhances data availability and reliability. By understanding the different types of replication and how to set it up, you can effectively distribute your database workload and improve overall performance.

SHARDING

Sharding is a database architecture pattern used to scale databases horizontally by splitting data across multiple database instances. This technique allows you to manage large datasets more efficiently and improves performance by distributing the load across multiple servers. In this section, we will explore what sharding is, its benefits, strategies for implementation, and best practices.

1. WHAT IS SHARDING?

Sharding involves partitioning a database into smaller, more manageable pieces called shards. Each shard is a separate database instance that contains a portion of the overall data. This approach allows you to spread the data and the workload, enhancing performance and reducing the chances of bottlenecks.

2. BENEFITS OF SHARDING

2.1 Improved Performance

By distributing data across multiple servers, sharding can significantly improve read and write performance. Each shard can handle a portion of the workload, reducing the load on any single database instance.

2.2 Increased Scalability

Sharding allows you to scale your database horizontally. As your data grows, you can add more shards to accommodate the increased volume without affecting the performance of existing shards.

2.3 Enhanced Availability

With sharding, you can improve availability and fault tolerance. If one shard goes down, the others can continue to function, ensuring that your application remains operational.

3. SHARDING STRATEGIES

There are several strategies for implementing sharding, and the choice depends on your specific use case and requirements:

3.1 Horizontal Sharding

Horizontal sharding involves splitting data across shards based on certain criteria, such as user ID or geographical location. Each shard contains a subset of the data, which can be accessed independently. For example:

- Shard 1: Users 1 - 1000
- Shard 2: Users 1001 - 2000

3.2 Vertical Sharding

In vertical sharding, different database tables or functionalities are split across shards. For instance, user data might reside in one shard while order data is stored in another. This can be beneficial for applications with distinct data access patterns.

3.3 Directory-Based Sharding

This method uses a lookup table or directory to keep track of where data resides. When an application needs to access data, it queries the directory to find out which shard contains the relevant information. This approach adds a layer of complexity but offers flexibility in shard management.

3.4 Hash-Based Sharding

In hash-based sharding, a hash function determines the shard for a specific piece of data. This ensures a uniform distribution of data across shards but may require additional overhead to manage the hash function.

4. IMPLEMENTING SHARDING IN MYSQL

4.1 Define the Sharding Key

The first step in implementing sharding is to determine the sharding key. This key is the attribute used to decide how to partition the data across shards. Choose a key that evenly distributes the data to avoid hotspots.

4.2 Create Shards

Set up separate MySQL instances for each shard. Each shard should have a consistent schema to ensure that the application can interact with them seamlessly.

4.3 Application Logic

Modify your application logic to route requests to the appropriate shard based on the sharding key. This may involve maintaining a mapping of shard locations and implementing logic to handle read and write operations across shards.

4.4 Data Migration

If you're sharding an existing database, plan for data migration. You may need to migrate data from a monolithic database to the newly created shards while minimizing downtime.

5. BEST PRACTICES FOR SHARDING

Choose the Right Sharding Key: Select a sharding key that provides even distribution of data and minimizes the risk of hotspots.

Monitor Performance: Regularly monitor the performance of each shard to identify potential bottlenecks and redistribute data if necessary.

Implement Load Balancing: Use load balancing techniques to distribute requests evenly across shards and improve performance.

Consider Complexity: Be mindful of the added complexity that comes with sharding. Ensure that your team is equipped to manage and maintain a sharded architecture.

Sharding is an effective strategy for managing large datasets and scaling databases in a MySQL environment. By understanding the different sharding strategies and implementing best practices, you can enhance the performance and scalability of your applications.

DATABASE SECURITY

In today's digital landscape, safeguarding your data is paramount. Database security involves protecting your database from unauthorized access, breaches, and vulnerabilities. This section will cover essential security measures and best practices to ensure your MySQL databases remain secure.

1. UNDERSTANDING DATABASE SECURITY

Database security encompasses a wide range of practices aimed at ensuring the confidentiality, integrity, and availability of data. Given the increasing sophistication of cyber threats, implementing robust security measures is essential for protecting sensitive information.

2. KEY SECURITY CONCEPTS

2.1 Confidentiality

Confidentiality ensures that only authorized users can access sensitive data. This involves implementing strict access controls and user authentication mechanisms.

2.2 Integrity

Integrity guarantees that data remains accurate and unaltered during storage and transmission. Measures should be in place to prevent unauthorized modifications and to validate data integrity.

2.3 Availability

Availability ensures that authorized users can access the database and its data when needed. This includes implementing backup and recovery plans to prevent data loss.

3. BEST PRACTICES FOR DATABASE SECURITY

3.1 Use Strong Passwords

Enforce strong password policies for database users. Passwords should be complex, combining letters, numbers, and special characters. Regularly update passwords and encourage users to avoid sharing their credentials.

3.2 Implement Role-Based Access Control (RBAC)

Role-based access control allows you to grant users permissions based on their roles within the organization. This minimizes the risk of unauthorized access by ensuring that users only have the permissions necessary for their job functions.

3.3 Secure Connections

Use SSL/TLS to encrypt data in transit between the database server and clients. This prevents unauthorized interception of sensitive information during transmission.

3.4 Regularly Update and Patch

Keep your MySQL server and associated applications up to date with the latest security patches and updates. This helps protect against known vulnerabilities and exploits.

3.5 Audit and Monitor Activity

Implement auditing and logging to track database access and changes. Regularly review logs to identify unusual activity, which may indicate unauthorized access or breaches.

3.6 Limit User Privileges

Follow the principle of least privilege by granting users only the permissions they need to perform their job. Regularly review user accounts and permissions to remove any unnecessary access.

3.7 Backup Data Regularly

Regular backups are essential for data recovery in case of data loss or corruption. Store backups securely, and test the restoration process periodically to ensure data integrity.

3.8 Secure Configuration

Review and secure the MySQL configuration file to disable unnecessary features and services. This reduces the attack surface and limits potential vulnerabilities.

3.9 Use Firewalls and Network Security

Implement firewalls to restrict access to the database server. Only allow connections from trusted IP addresses and networks. Consider using Virtual Private Networks (VPNs) for secure remote access.

4. ENCRYPTION

4.1 Data Encryption at Rest

Encrypt sensitive data stored within the database to protect it from unauthorized access. MySQL supports data encryption through functions like AES_ENCRYPT and by enabling Transparent Data Encryption (TDE) for entire tablespaces.

4.2 Data Encryption in Transit

Ensure that data transmitted between the client and server is encrypted using SSL/TLS. This protects against eavesdropping and man-in-the-middle attacks.

5. INCIDENT RESPONSE PLAN

Having an incident response plan is crucial for effectively addressing security breaches or data leaks. Establish procedures for identifying, responding to, and recovering from security incidents. Regularly train your team on these protocols to ensure everyone knows their roles in the event of a breach.

Database security is an ongoing process that requires continuous attention and adaptation to emerging threats. By implementing the best practices outlined in this section, you can significantly enhance the security of your MySQL databases.

DATA ENCRYPTION

Data encryption is a critical aspect of database security that helps protect sensitive information from unauthorized access. In this section, we will explore the importance of encryption in MySQL, the methods available for encrypting data, and best practices for implementing encryption.

1. UNDERSTANDING DATA ENCRYPTION

Encryption transforms readable data into an unreadable format, making it incomprehensible to unauthorized users. Only those with the appropriate decryption keys can convert the data back to its original form. This ensures that even if the data is intercepted or accessed without authorization, it remains protected.

2. TYPES OF DATA ENCRYPTION

2.1 Data at Rest

Data at rest refers to inactive data stored physically in any digital form (e.g., databases, data warehouses). Protecting this data is essential, as it can be vulnerable to theft if proper security measures are not in place.

- **MySQL Transparent Data Encryption (TDE):** MySQL provides TDE, which automatically encrypts data files on disk without requiring changes to the application. This feature helps secure sensitive information without impacting performance or usability.

2.2 Data in Transit

Data in transit refers to data actively moving from one location to another, such as across networks or between servers. Protecting this data is crucial to prevent interception during transmission.

- **SSL/TLS Encryption:** MySQL supports SSL/TLS for encrypting data transmitted between the database server and clients. By enabling SSL, you can ensure that all communication is secure, preventing eavesdropping and tampering.

3. ENCRYPTION METHODS IN MYSQL

3.1 Built-in Encryption Functions

MySQL offers several built-in functions to facilitate data encryption and decryption:

AES_ENCRYPT: This function encrypts a string using the Advanced Encryption Standard (AES). For example:

```
SELECT AES_ENCRYPT('sensitive_data', 'encryption_key') AS encrypted_data;
```

AES_DECRYPT: This function decrypts data encrypted with AES. For example:

```
SELECT AES_DECRYPT(encrypted_data, 'encryption_key') AS decrypted_data;
```

Creating Encrypted Columns

You can create encrypted columns in your tables to store sensitive data securely. Here's how to do it:

```
CREATE TABLE users (

    id INT PRIMARY KEY,

    name VARCHAR(100),

    email VARBINARY(255) -- Use VARBINARY for encrypted data

);
```

When inserting data, use the AES_ENCRYPT function to store the encrypted value:

```
INSERT INTO users (id, name, email) VALUES (1, 'John Doe', AES_ENCRYPT('john@example.com', 'encryption_key'));
```

4. BEST PRACTICES FOR DATA ENCRYPTION

4.1 Use Strong Encryption Keys

Always use strong and complex encryption keys to enhance security. Avoid using easily guessable keys and regularly change them to mitigate risks.

4.2 Limit Access to Encryption Keys

Access to encryption keys should be restricted to authorized personnel only. Use secure key management practices to protect keys from unauthorized access or exposure.

4.3 Monitor and Audit

Regularly monitor and audit encrypted data and key management practices. This helps identify any potential security vulnerabilities and ensures compliance with regulatory requirements.

4.4 Test Your Encryption

Regularly test your encryption implementation to ensure it is functioning correctly. This includes verifying that encrypted data can be decrypted successfully and assessing the performance impact of encryption.

Data encryption is a fundamental component of database security, protecting sensitive information from unauthorized access and potential breaches. By implementing robust encryption practices in MySQL, you can significantly enhance the security of your data.

PERFORMANCE SCHEMA

The Performance Schema is a powerful feature of MySQL that provides insights into the performance characteristics of your database system. It helps you monitor and optimize MySQL performance by collecting performance metrics and statistics in real-time. In this section, we will explore the key components of the Performance Schema, how to enable it, and how to utilize its capabilities for performance tuning.

1. WHAT IS PERFORMANCE SCHEMA?

The Performance Schema is a set of tables that store information about server execution at a low level. It provides a comprehensive view of various server metrics, including:

- Resource usage (CPU, memory, disk I/O)
- Wait events (locks, I/O operations)
- Query execution times
- Statement-level and transaction-level metrics

2. ENABLING PERFORMANCE SCHEMA

By default, the Performance Schema is enabled in MySQL installations. However, if it is not enabled or you want to customize its configuration, follow these steps:

Edit the MySQL configuration file (my.cnf **or** my.ini**):**

[mysqld]

performance_schema=ON

Restart the MySQL server to apply the changes.

You can verify if the Performance Schema is enabled by executing:

SHOW VARIABLES LIKE 'performance_schema';

3. KEY TABLES IN PERFORMANCE SCHEMA

The Performance Schema consists of several important tables that capture various performance metrics. Here are a few key tables:

events_waits_summary_by_instance: This table provides a summary of wait events by instance, helping you identify bottlenecks caused by waiting on resources.

events_statements_summary_by_digest: This table summarizes statement execution, allowing you to analyze the performance of different query types based on their digest.

threads: This table contains information about the threads that are currently running on the server, including their state and resource consumption.

You can query these tables to gather insights into your database performance. For example:

SELECT * FROM events_statements_summary_by_digest ORDER BY count_star DESC LIMIT 10;

4. ANALYZING PERFORMANCE METRICS

Using the Performance Schema, you can analyze various performance metrics to identify areas for improvement. Here are a few common analysis techniques:

4.1 Monitoring Wait Events

Wait events indicate how long threads wait for resources. By monitoring these events, you can identify potential bottlenecks. For example:

SELECT EVENT_NAME, SUM(TIMER_WAIT) AS total_wait_time

FROM events_waits_summary_by_instance

GROUP BY EVENT_NAME

ORDER BY total_wait_time DESC;

4.2 Analyzing Query Performance

Understanding query performance is essential for optimization. You can analyze the most frequently executed queries using:

SELECT DIGEST_TEXT, COUNT_STAR, SUM_TIMER_WAIT

FROM events_statements_summary_by_digest

ORDER BY COUNT_STAR DESC

LIMIT 10;

4.3 Tracking Resource Usage

You can track resource usage over time to identify trends and potential issues. For instance, to analyze memory usage:

SELECT * FROM performance_schema.memory_summary_global_by_event_name;

5. BEST PRACTICES FOR USING PERFORMANCE SCHEMA

5.1 Limit Overhead

While the Performance Schema is designed to have minimal overhead, consider enabling only the necessary instruments and consumers to reduce impact on performance. You can configure this in the MySQL configuration file.

5.2 Regularly Review Metrics

Make it a habit to regularly review the metrics collected by the Performance Schema. This will help you identify and address performance issues proactively.

5.3 Combine with Other Tools

While the Performance Schema provides valuable insights, consider combining it with other monitoring tools (like MySQL Enterprise Monitor, Percona Monitoring and Management) for a comprehensive performance overview.

The Performance Schema is an invaluable tool for monitoring and optimizing MySQL performance. By understanding how to leverage its features, you can gain deep insights into your database's behavior and make informed decisions to improve efficiency and performance.

USE QUERY CACHE

The Query Cache in MySQL is a powerful feature that can significantly improve the performance of your database by reducing the number of times it has to execute the same query. By caching the results of previously executed queries, MySQL can quickly retrieve the results from memory instead of re-executing the query against the database. In this section, we will explore how to enable and utilize the Query Cache effectively.

1. WHAT IS QUERY CACHE?

The Query Cache stores the results of SELECT statements and can return these results directly from the cache if the same query is executed again. The cache only stores the results of queries that do not modify data (i.e., SELECT queries), making it ideal for read-heavy workloads where the same queries are executed multiple times.

2. ENABLING QUERY CACHE

In MySQL, the Query Cache is disabled by default in some versions, so you may need to enable it. Here's how to do that:

Edit the MySQL configuration file (my.cnf **or** my.ini**):**

[mysqld]

query_cache_type = 1   # Enable the Query Cache

query_cache_size = 1048576 # Set the cache size to 1MB

Restart the MySQL server to apply the changes.

You can verify if the Query Cache is enabled by executing:

SHOW VARIABLES LIKE 'query_cache_size';

SHOW VARIABLES LIKE 'query_cache_type';

3. QUERY CACHE STRATEGIES

To effectively use the Query Cache, consider the following strategies:

3.1 Choosing Cachable Queries

Not all queries can be cached. The following criteria determine whether a query is cachable:

- The query must be a SELECT statement.
- The query should not contain any non-deterministic functions (like NOW() or RAND()).
- The table referenced in the query should not be updated after the query is executed.

3.2 Adjusting Cache Size

The size of the Query Cache can significantly impact its effectiveness. If the cache is too small, it may frequently evict cached results, leading to inefficiencies. Conversely, a larger cache may lead to increased memory usage. Monitor the performance and adjust the query_cache_size parameter accordingly.

4. QUERY CACHE MANAGEMENT

4.1 Using Query Cache Hints

You can use query cache hints to control how specific queries are cached. For example, you can force a query to be cached or ignored using the following syntax:

To cache a specific query:

SELECT SQL_CACHE column1, column2 FROM table_name WHERE condition;

To prevent caching of a specific query:

SELECT SQL_NO_CACHE column1, column2 FROM table_name WHERE condition;

4.2 Flushing the Query Cache

If you need to clear the Query Cache, you can use the following command:

RESET QUERY CACHE;

This command removes all cached results and is useful if you have made significant changes to the underlying data.

5. MONITORING QUERY CACHE

To monitor the effectiveness of the Query Cache, you can query the SHOW STATUS command to view relevant statistics:

SHOW STATUS LIKE 'Qcache%';

This will provide you with metrics such as:

- **Qcache_hits:** Number of times a query result was served from the cache.
- **Qcache_inserts:** Number of times a query result was added to the cache.
- **Qcache_lowmem_prunes:** Number of times cache entries were removed due to insufficient memory.

6. BEST PRACTICES FOR USING QUERY CACHE

6.1 Regularly Review Cache Performance

Continuously monitor the performance of your Query Cache. Analyze the statistics gathered from the SHOW STATUS command to determine if the cache is effective or if it requires adjustments.

6.2 Limit Use on Write-Heavy Workloads

Be cautious when using the Query Cache on write-heavy workloads. The cache will be invalidated whenever a table is modified, which may lead to more overhead than performance gains. In such scenarios, you may consider disabling the cache.

6.3 Optimize Queries

Ensure that the queries being executed are optimized for caching. Avoid using non-deterministic functions and ensure that they are well-structured for maximum cache efficiency.

The Query Cache is a valuable feature that can enhance the performance of your MySQL database by reducing the execution time of repeated queries. By understanding how to enable and manage the Query Cache effectively, you can make your database applications faster and more responsive.

AUDIT LOGGING

Audit logging is an essential feature for any database management system, including MySQL. It allows you to track and record database activities, providing visibility into changes made to your database. This capability is crucial for maintaining security, ensuring compliance, and troubleshooting issues. In this section, we will explore what audit logging is, how to implement it in MySQL, and best practices for using audit logs effectively.

1. WHAT IS AUDIT LOGGING?

Audit logging involves creating a record of actions taken within a database system. These logs can include details such as:

- **User Actions:** Who performed the action and when it occurred.
- **Executed Queries:** The actual SQL statements executed.
- **Affected Rows:** Information about which rows were changed, if applicable.
- **Connection Details:** Information about the session or connection used for the action.

By tracking these activities, audit logs help you maintain accountability and transparency in your database operations.

2. ENABLE AUDIT LOGGING IN MYSQL

To enable audit logging in MySQL, you can use the MySQL Enterprise Edition's Audit Plugin or set up general logging as a simpler alternative. Here's how to do both:

2.1 Using the MySQL Enterprise Audit Plugin

The MySQL Enterprise Audit Plugin provides a more comprehensive auditing solution. To enable it:

Install the Audit Plugin: Ensure the audit plugin is installed and enabled by executing:

INSTALL PLUGIN audit_log SONAME 'audit_log.so';

Configure the Plugin: Update your MySQL configuration file (my.cnf or my.ini) with the necessary settings:

[mysqld]

audit_log_policy = ALL # or 'LOGINS' or 'NONE'

audit_log_file = /var/log/mysql/audit.log

Restart MySQL Server: Restart the MySQL server to apply the changes.

2.2 Using General Query Logging

For a simpler setup, you can use the general query log, which logs all SQL statements received by the server:

Enable General Query Logging: Update the MySQL configuration file:

[mysqld]

general_log = 1

general_log_file = /var/log/mysql/general.log

Restart MySQL Server: Restart the server to enable logging.

Monitor Logs: You can monitor the general log to see all executed queries.

3. ANALYZING AUDIT LOGS

Once audit logging is enabled, you can analyze the logs to gain insights into database activities. Audit logs are typically stored in plain text files, making them easy to read and analyze using standard text-processing tools.

3.1 Using SQL Queries

If you're using general logs, you can load the log file into a temporary table for analysis:

```
CREATE TABLE temp_log (id INT AUTO_INCREMENT PRIMARY KEY, log_entry TEXT);

LOAD DATA INFILE '/var/log/mysql/general.log' INTO TABLE temp_log;
```

Then, you can query the temp_log table to filter and analyze the entries:

```sql
SELECT * FROM temp_log WHERE log_entry LIKE '%UPDATE%';
```

4. BEST PRACTICES FOR AUDIT LOGGING

4.1 Regular Log Review

Regularly review your audit logs to identify any suspicious activities or patterns. Implement automated monitoring tools that alert you of unusual behavior.

4.2 Log Retention Policy

Establish a log retention policy that defines how long logs will be kept and when they should be archived or deleted. This helps manage storage space and ensures compliance with data protection regulations.

4.3 Secure Log Storage

Ensure that your audit logs are stored securely. Use appropriate file permissions to restrict access to authorized personnel only. Consider encrypting log files to protect sensitive information.

4.4 Optimize Log Settings

Evaluate and adjust your logging settings based on your environment's requirements. For example, if you have a high-traffic database, consider logging only critical events instead of all queries to reduce log size.

Audit logging is a vital component of database security and compliance. By enabling audit logging in MySQL, you can track user activities, analyze changes, and ensure accountability within your database environment.

AVOID SELECT *

When working with SQL databases, it's common to see queries that use SELECT *. While this may seem convenient, especially for beginners, there are several important reasons to avoid using SELECT * in your queries. In this section, we will discuss why it's crucial to specify columns instead of using SELECT *, and how doing so can improve the performance and maintainability of your SQL code.

1. WHAT IS SELECT * ?

The SELECT * statement retrieves all columns from a specified table. For example:

SELECT * FROM employees;

This query returns every column for every row in the employees table, regardless of whether you need all that data or not.

2. REASONS TO AVOID SELECT *

2.1 PERFORMANCE ISSUES

When you use SELECT *, the database retrieves all columns from the table, which can lead to several performance-related issues:

Increased Data Transfer: If your table has many columns, sending all that data over the network can consume more bandwidth and slow down response times. This is especially critical in high-traffic applications.

Slow Query Execution: Retrieving unnecessary columns can increase the time it takes to execute the query, leading to slower application performance.

2.2 REDUCED CLARITY

Using SELECT * can make your SQL queries less clear. When you explicitly specify the columns you need, it becomes easier for others (and yourself) to understand what data the query is retrieving. This enhances readability and maintainability.

For example:

SELECT first_name, last_name, email FROM employees;

This query clearly indicates which specific data is being retrieved, making it easier for others to understand the intent.

2.3 POTENTIAL SCHEMA CHANGES

If the underlying table schema changes—such as adding or removing columns—using SELECT * can lead to unexpected results:

New Columns: If a new column is added, your application may start receiving data it doesn't expect or handle, potentially leading to errors or bugs.

Removed Columns: If a column is removed, queries using SELECT * may fail or return incomplete data.

3. WHEN TO USE SELECT *

While it's generally advisable to avoid SELECT *, there are scenarios where it may be acceptable, such as:

Ad-hoc Queries: For quick tests or exploratory queries where you need to see all data without concern for performance or clarity.

Debugging: When troubleshooting, and you want to inspect the entire dataset quickly.

However, these situations should be exceptions rather than the rule.

4. BEST PRACTICES

4.1 SPECIFY COLUMNS

Always specify the columns you need in your queries. This practice improves performance, clarity, and maintainability. For example:

SELECT id, first_name, last_name FROM employees WHERE department_id = 3;

4.2 USE ALIASES

When working with multiple tables or complex queries, use aliases for better readability:

SELECT e.id AS employee_id, e.first_name, d.name AS department_name

FROM employees AS e

JOIN departments AS d ON e.department_id = d.id;

4.3 LIMIT DATA RETRIEVAL

If you're working with large datasets, consider using the LIMIT clause to restrict the number of rows returned:

SELECT first_name, last_name FROM employees LIMIT 100;

Avoiding SELECT * is a best practice in SQL development that can lead to improved performance, enhanced clarity, and better adaptability to changes in your database schema. By specifying the columns you need, you ensure that your queries are efficient and easy to understand.

MANAGING DATABASE USERS AND ROLES

In any relational database management system (RDBMS), managing users and their permissions is critical to maintaining security, integrity, and proper access control. In this section, we will explore how to create, manage, and assign roles to users in MySQL. This includes granting and revoking permissions, ensuring that users only have access to the data they need, and promoting best practices for user management.

1. UNDERSTANDING DATABASE USERS AND ROLES

1.1 DATABASE USERS

A database user is an account that has been granted access to a MySQL database. Each user can have different permissions that determine what operations they can perform within the database, such as reading, writing, updating, or deleting data.

1.2 ROLES

Roles are a way to group permissions. Instead of assigning permissions to individual users, you can create a role with a specific set of permissions and then assign that role to one or more users. This simplifies user management and helps ensure consistency across users with similar responsibilities.

2. CREATING USERS

To create a new user in MySQL, you use the CREATE USER statement. Here's the basic syntax:

CREATE USER 'username'@'host' IDENTIFIED BY 'password';

Example:

CREATE USER 'john_doe'@'localhost' IDENTIFIED BY 'securePassword123';

In this example, we created a user named john_doe who can connect from the local host with the specified password.

3. GRANTING PERMISSIONS

After creating a user, you need to grant them the necessary permissions. This can be done using the GRANT statement. The syntax is as follows:

GRANT privilege_type ON database_name.table_name TO 'username'@'host';

Example

To grant SELECT and INSERT permissions on a specific table:

```
GRANT    SELECT,    INSERT    ON    sales.transactions    TO
'john_doe'@'localhost';
```

To grant all privileges on a specific database:

```
GRANT ALL PRIVILEGES ON sales.* TO 'john_doe'@'localhost';
```

4. CREATING AND MANAGING ROLES

4.1 CREATING A ROLE

In MySQL, you can create a role using the CREATE ROLE statement. The syntax is straightforward:

```
CREATE ROLE 'role_name';
```

Example

```
CREATE ROLE 'sales_representative';
```

4.2 GRANTING PERMISSIONS TO A ROLE

Once a role is created, you can assign specific privileges to that role:

```
GRANT    SELECT,    INSERT    ON    sales.transactions    TO
'sales_representative';
```

4.3 ASSIGNING A ROLE TO A USER

To assign a role to a user, use the GRANT statement again:

```
GRANT 'role_name' TO 'username'@'host';
```

Example

GRANT 'sales_representative' TO 'john_doe'@'localhost';

5. REVOKING PERMISSIONS

If you need to remove a user's permissions or revoke a role from a user, you can use the REVOKE statement:

Example

To revoke specific privileges:

REVOKE INSERT ON sales.transactions FROM 'john_doe'@'localhost';

To revoke a role:

REVOKE 'sales_representative' FROM 'john_doe'@'localhost';

6. DELETING USERS

If a user no longer needs access to the database, you can delete their account using the DROP USER statement:

Example

DROP USER 'john_doe'@'localhost';

7. BEST PRACTICES FOR USER MANAGEMENT

Least Privilege Principle: Always grant users the minimum permissions necessary to perform their job functions. This minimizes security risks.

Use Roles: Create roles to group permissions and assign them to users instead of managing individual user permissions.

Regular Audits: Periodically review user accounts and permissions to ensure they are up-to-date and relevant.

Strong Password Policies: Enforce strong password policies for users to enhance security.

Managing database users and roles is essential for maintaining security and ensuring that users can perform their tasks effectively without exposing sensitive data or systems to unnecessary risk. By implementing proper user management practices, you can create a secure and efficient environment for your MySQL databases.

ANALYZING SLOW QUERIES

In database management, performance is key to ensuring that applications run smoothly and efficiently. One of the most common performance issues that database administrators face is slow queries. In this section, we will explore how to identify, analyze, and optimize slow queries in MySQL.

1. UNDERSTANDING SLOW QUERIES

Slow queries are SQL statements that take longer than expected to execute. They can significantly impact the performance of your database and, by extension, your application. Identifying these queries is essential for maintaining a responsive database environment.

2. ENABLING SLOW QUERY LOGGING

MySQL has a built-in feature to log slow queries, which can help you identify performance bottlenecks. To enable the slow query log, you need to modify the MySQL configuration file (my.cnf or my.ini) and set the following parameters:

[mysqld]

slow_query_log = ON

slow_query_log_file = /var/log/mysql/slow-query.log

long_query_time = 2

In this example, slow queries that take longer than 2 seconds will be logged. After making these changes, restart the MySQL server for the settings to take effect.

3. ANALYZING SLOW QUERY LOGS

Once slow query logging is enabled, you can analyze the generated log file. The slow query log provides valuable information, including the SQL statement, execution time, lock time, number of rows examined, and number of rows sent.

3.1 USING mysqldumpslow

MySQL provides a utility called mysqldumpslow that summarizes the slow query log, making it easier to identify problem queries. The basic usage is:

mysqldumpslow /var/log/mysql/slow-query.log

You can use various options to customize the output, such as:

- -t N: Show the top N queries.
- -s: Sort the output by various fields (e.g., query time).
- -g pattern: Show only queries matching the specified pattern.

Example

mysqldumpslow -t 10 -s t /var/log/mysql/slow-query.log

This command will display the top 10 slowest queries from the log, sorted by execution time.

4. USING EXPLAIN TO ANALYZE QUERY PLANS

To further analyze slow queries, you can use the EXPLAIN statement. This command provides information about how MySQL executes a query, including the tables accessed, the order of access, and any indexes used.

Syntax

EXPLAIN SELECT * FROM your_table WHERE conditions;

Example

```
EXPLAIN SELECT * FROM orders WHERE customer_id = 123;
```

The output will include fields such as:

- **id**: The identifier of the query.
- **select_type**: The type of query (e.g., SIMPLE, PRIMARY).
- **table**: The table being accessed.
- **type**: The join type (e.g., ALL, index, range).
- **possible_keys**: Any possible indexes that could be used.
- **key**: The actual index used.
- **rows**: The number of rows examined.

By analyzing this output, you can identify whether the query can be optimized further.

5. OPTIMIZING SLOW QUERIES

5.1 USE INDEXES

One of the most effective ways to improve query performance is to use indexes. Ensure that the columns used in WHERE, JOIN, and ORDER BY clauses are properly indexed.

5.2 AVOID SELECT *

Instead of using SELECT *, specify only the columns you need. This reduces the amount of data retrieved and can speed up query execution.

5.3 REWRITE QUERIES

Sometimes, rewriting a query can lead to performance improvements. For example, use INNER JOIN instead of

OUTER JOIN if possible, and avoid subqueries that can be replaced with joins.

5.4 ANALYZE AND OPTIMIZE TABLES

Use the ANALYZE TABLE command to update the table statistics, which helps the MySQL optimizer make better decisions.

ANALYZE TABLE your_table;

6. MONITORING QUERY PERFORMANCE

Once you have optimized slow queries, it's crucial to monitor their performance continually. MySQL provides various tools and features for monitoring, such as:

Performance Schema: A feature that provides a way to inspect the performance of various database components.

SHOW PROCESSLIST: This command shows the currently running queries and their statuses.

Analyzing slow queries is a vital aspect of database management. By enabling slow query logging, using tools like mysqldumpslow and EXPLAIN, and implementing optimization techniques, you can significantly improve the performance of your MySQL database.

OPTIMIZING JOINs

JOIN operations are essential in relational databases, allowing you to combine rows from two or more tables based on a related column. However, poorly optimized JOINs can lead to performance issues, especially as the size of your data grows. In this section, we will explore techniques for optimizing JOIN operations in MySQL to enhance performance and efficiency.

1. UNDERSTANDING JOIN TYPES

Before optimizing JOINs, it's essential to understand the different types of JOINs:

- **INNER JOIN**: Returns records that have matching values in both tables.
- **LEFT JOIN (or LEFT OUTER JOIN)**: Returns all records from the left table and matched records from the right table. If no match is found, NULL values are returned for columns from the right table.
- **RIGHT JOIN (or RIGHT OUTER JOIN)**: Returns all records from the right table and matched records from the left table. If no match is found, NULL values are returned for columns from the left table.
- **FULL JOIN (or FULL OUTER JOIN)**: Returns records when there is a match in either left or right table records. (Note: MySQL does not support FULL OUTER JOIN directly, but you can achieve it using a UNION of LEFT and RIGHT JOINs.)

2. USE INDEXES

One of the most effective ways to optimize JOINs is by using indexes on the columns involved in the JOIN condition. Proper indexing can significantly reduce the time required to locate and combine rows from different tables.

Example

If you have two tables, orders and customers, and you often join them on customer_id, ensure that both tables have an index on the customer_id column:

CREATE INDEX idx_customer_id ON customers(customer_id);

CREATE   INDEX   idx_order_customer_id   ON orders(customer_id);

3. LIMIT THE NUMBER OF JOINs

While JOINs are powerful, excessive JOINs can lead to complex queries that are difficult to optimize. Limit the number of JOINs in a single query to only those that are necessary. If you find yourself joining many tables, consider breaking down the query into smaller, manageable parts.

4. SELECT ONLY NECESSARY COLUMNS

Instead of using SELECT *, specify only the columns you need in the result set. This practice reduces the amount of data transferred and processed, leading to faster execution times.

Example

Instead of:

SELECT * FROM orders

INNER JOIN customers ON orders.customer_id = customers.customer_id;

Use:

SELECT orders.order_id, customers.customer_name

FROM orders

INNER JOIN customers ON orders.customer_id = customers.customer_id;

5. USE THE MOST RESTRICTIVE JOIN FIRST

When using multiple JOINs, the order in which they are executed can affect performance. MySQL's optimizer will usually determine the best execution plan, but you can help it by placing the most restrictive JOINs (those that filter out the most rows) first in your query.

Example

If you have an INNER JOIN that narrows down a large dataset, consider placing it before a LEFT JOIN that may return more data.

6. AVOID JOINING ON NON-INDEXED COLUMNS

Ensure that you are joining on columns that are indexed. Joining on non-indexed columns can lead to a full table scan, significantly slowing down query execution.

7. ANALYZE YOUR QUERIES

Use the EXPLAIN statement to analyze how MySQL executes your JOIN queries. The output will provide insights into the execution plan, including which indexes are used and how many rows are scanned.

Example

EXPLAIN SELECT orders.order_id, customers.customer_name

FROM orders

INNER JOIN customers ON orders.customer_id = customers.customer_id;

Review the output to identify potential performance bottlenecks and optimize your query accordingly.

Optimizing JOINs is crucial for enhancing the performance of your MySQL database. By using indexes, limiting the number of JOINs, selecting only necessary columns, and analyzing your queries, you can significantly improve query execution times.

DATABASE DESIGN

Database design is a critical step in developing a robust, efficient, and scalable database system. A well-designed database can significantly improve application performance, ensure data integrity, and simplify maintenance. In this section, we will explore the key principles of database design and best practices for creating an effective MySQL database.

1. UNDERSTAND REQUIREMENTS

Before diving into design, it's essential to understand the requirements of your application. Engage with stakeholders to gather insights on:

- **Data Requirements**: What data needs to be stored? What are the relationships between different data entities?
- **Performance Needs**: What are the expected query patterns and transaction volumes? Will the database need to handle heavy read or write operations?
- **Future Growth**: Consider potential future requirements, such as scalability, data retention, and reporting needs.

2. IDENTIFY ENTITIES AND RELATIONSHIPS

Once you have a clear understanding of the requirements, identify the entities (tables) you need to create. Each entity should represent a distinct object or concept in your application. For example, in an e-commerce application, entities may include:

- Customers
- Products
- Orders
- Order Items

Next, define the relationships between these entities. Common relationship types include:

- **One-to-One**: A single record in one table is linked to a single record in another table (e.g., a user profile and a user account).
- **One-to-Many**: A single record in one table is linked to multiple records in another table (e.g., a customer and their orders).
- **Many-to-Many**: Multiple records in one table can relate to multiple records in another table (e.g., products and categories).

For many-to-many relationships, create a junction table that holds the foreign keys from both related tables.

3. CHOOSE THE RIGHT DATA TYPES

Selecting appropriate data types for each column is crucial for optimizing storage and performance. Consider the following:

- **Numeric Types**: Choose the smallest type that can accommodate your data (e.g., use TINYINT for small integers and BIGINT for larger values).
- **String Types**: Use VARCHAR for variable-length strings and CHAR for fixed-length strings. Consider the length of the data you expect to store.
- **Date and Time Types**: Use DATE, TIME, or DATETIME for storing date and time information.
- **JSON**: Use the JSON data type for semi-structured data when necessary.

4. NORMATIZATION

Normalization is the process of organizing data to reduce redundancy and improve data integrity. The main goals of normalization are:

- Ensure that each piece of data is stored in only one place (no duplicate data).
- Reduce data anomalies during insertions, updates, and deletions.

Normal Forms

There are several normal forms, each with specific rules. The most commonly used are:

- **First Normal Form (1NF)**: Ensures that each column contains atomic values (no repeating groups).
- **Second Normal Form (2NF)**: Achieved when a table is in 1NF and all non-key attributes are fully functionally dependent on the primary key.
- **Third Normal Form (3NF)**: Achieved when a table is in 2NF and all attributes are only dependent on the primary key (no transitive dependencies).

5. DENORMALIZATION (WHEN NECESSARY)

While normalization is essential for data integrity, sometimes denormalization is necessary to improve query performance. Denormalization involves combining tables or adding redundant data to reduce the number of JOINs required in queries.

Use denormalization judiciously, as it can lead to data anomalies and increase storage requirements.

6. DEFINE PRIMARY AND FOREIGN KEYS

Assign primary keys to each table to uniquely identify each record. A primary key can be a single column or a combination of columns (composite key).

Foreign keys are used to establish relationships between tables. They enforce referential integrity, ensuring that a record in one table corresponds to a valid record in another table.

Example

In an orders table, you might define a foreign key to reference the customer table:

CREATE TABLE customers (

   customer_id INT PRIMARY KEY,

   customer_name VARCHAR(100) NOT NULL

);

CREATE TABLE orders (

   order_id INT PRIMARY KEY,

   customer_id INT,

   order_date DATETIME,

FOREIGN   KEY   (customer_id)   REFERENCES customers(customer_id)

);

7. DOCUMENT YOUR DESIGN

As you design your database, document the schema, relationships, and any important decisions made during the design process. This documentation will serve as a valuable reference for developers, DBAs, and stakeholders, ensuring that everyone understands the structure and logic behind the database.

Effective database design is foundational to creating a successful application. By understanding requirements, identifying entities and relationships, choosing the right data types, normalizing data, defining keys, and documenting your design, you can create a MySQL database that is efficient, scalable, and easy to maintain.

USE CONNECTION POOLING

Connection pooling is a technique used to enhance the performance of database applications by managing the connections to the database more efficiently. Rather than opening and closing a database connection for each request, connection pooling allows multiple requests to share a limited number of connections, reducing the overhead associated with establishing and terminating database connections.

1. WHAT IS CONNECTION POOLING?

A connection pool is a collection of database connections that are created and managed by a connection pool manager. When an application needs to interact with the database, it requests a connection from the pool. After the operations are completed, the connection is returned to the pool for reuse. This approach offers several advantages:

- **Improved Performance**: By reusing existing connections, the application avoids the overhead of establishing a new connection each time a database operation is required.
- **Resource Management**: Connection pooling helps to limit the number of active connections to the database, preventing resource exhaustion and maintaining stability.
- **Faster Response Times**: Since obtaining a connection from the pool is quicker than establishing a new one, applications can respond faster to user requests.

2. CONFIGURING CONNECTION POOLING IN MYSQL

When using MySQL, connection pooling can be implemented using various libraries and frameworks depending on your programming language or environment. Here, we'll cover a few popular options:

2.1 Using MySQL Connector/Python

For Python applications, you can use the mysql-connector-python library with a connection pool. Here's how to set it up:

Install the MySQL Connector:

```
pip install mysql-connector-python
```

Create a Connection Pool:

```
import mysql.connector

from mysql.connector import pooling


# Create a connection pool

pool = pooling.MySQLConnectionPool(

    pool_name="mypool",

    pool_size=5,

    host='localhost',

    user='your_user',

    password='your_password',

    database='your_database'

)
```

Using the Connection Pool:

```
# Get a connection from the pool

connection = pool.get_connection()
```

```python
try:

    cursor = connection.cursor()

    cursor.execute("SELECT * FROM your_table")

    results = cursor.fetchall()

    for row in results:

        print(row)

finally:

    cursor.close()

    connection.close()  # Returns the connection to the pool
```

2.2 Using Java with JDBC

If you are using Java, the HikariCP library is a popular choice for connection pooling with MySQL:

Add the HikariCP Dependency:

If you're using Maven, add the following dependency to your pom.xml:

```xml
<dependency>

    <groupId>com.zaxxer</groupId>
```

```
<artifactId>HikariCP</artifactId>

<version>5.0.1</version>

</dependency>
```

Configure HikariCP:

```java
import com.zaxxer.hikari.HikariConfig;

import com.zaxxer.hikari.HikariDataSource;


HikariConfig config = new HikariConfig();

config.setJdbcUrl("jdbc:mysql://localhost:3306/your_database");

config.setUsername("your_user");

config.setPassword("your_password");

config.setMaximumPoolSize(10);


HikariDataSource dataSource = new HikariDataSource(config);
```

Using the Connection Pool:

```java
try (Connection connection = dataSource.getConnection()) {
```

```
Statement statement = connection.createStatement();

ResultSet resultSet = statement.executeQuery("SELECT *
FROM your_table");

while (resultSet.next()) {

    System.out.println(resultSet.getString("your_column"));

}

} catch (SQLException e) {

    e.printStackTrace();

}
```

3. BEST PRACTICES FOR CONNECTION POOLING

To maximize the benefits of connection pooling, consider the following best practices:

Set an Appropriate Pool Size: The pool size should be based on the expected workload and the capacity of your MySQL server. Too many connections can lead to performance degradation, while too few can create bottlenecks.

Use Connection Timeout Settings: Configure timeout settings to avoid holding connections for too long. This helps to release idle connections and make them available for other requests.

Monitor Pool Usage: Keep track of connection pool metrics (e.g., active connections, idle connections) to identify potential issues and optimize performance.

Close Connections Properly: Always close connections when done, which returns them to the pool for reuse.

Connection pooling is an essential technique for optimizing database interactions in MySQL applications. By effectively managing database connections, applications can achieve improved performance, reduced latency, and better resource management.

UTILIZE MYSQL EVENTS

MySQL Events provide a way to schedule tasks that run automatically at specified intervals or times. This feature is particularly useful for automating repetitive tasks, such as cleanup operations, report generation, or regular data updates, without the need for external scripts or cron jobs. In this section, we will explore how to create, manage, and utilize MySQL Events effectively.

1. WHAT ARE MYSQL EVENTS?

MySQL Events are similar to stored procedures that are scheduled to execute automatically at predetermined times or intervals. They can be used for various purposes, such as:

- Automating regular database maintenance tasks (e.g., deleting old records, updating statistics).

- Performing data aggregations or transformations periodically.
- Sending notifications or alerts based on certain conditions.

2. ENABLING EVENT SCHEDULING

Before you can create and use events, you need to ensure that the Event Scheduler is enabled in your MySQL server. You can check its status with the following command:

SHOW VARIABLES LIKE 'event_scheduler';

If the Event Scheduler is disabled, you can enable it by executing:

SET GLOBAL event_scheduler = ON;

Alternatively, you can enable it permanently by adding the following line to your MySQL configuration file (e.g., my.cnf or my.ini):

event_scheduler=ON

3. CREATING AN EVENT

To create an event, you use the CREATE EVENT statement. The syntax is as follows:

CREATE EVENT event_name

ON SCHEDULE schedule

DO

  sql_statement;

3.1. Example of Creating an Event

Let's create a simple event that deletes records older than 30 days from a table named logs every day at midnight.

CREATE EVENT delete_old_logs

ON SCHEDULE EVERY 1 DAY

STARTS '2024-10-01 00:00:00'

DO

  DELETE FROM logs WHERE log_date < NOW() - INTERVAL 30 DAY;

3.2. Understanding the Schedule

In the above example:

- ON SCHEDULE EVERY 1 DAY specifies that the event will execute once every day.
- STARTS '2024-10-01 00:00:00' indicates when the event should start running.

4. ALTERING AND DROPPING EVENTS

You can modify or delete existing events using the ALTER EVENT and DROP EVENT statements.

4.1. Altering an Event

For instance, if you want to change the interval to run the event every hour, you can do so like this:

ALTER EVENT delete_old_logs

ON SCHEDULE EVERY 1 HOUR;

4.2. Dropping an Event

To remove an event, use the DROP EVENT statement:

DROP EVENT delete_old_logs;

5. VIEWING EVENTS

You can list all existing events in your database by querying the information_schema.EVENTS table:

SELECT EVENT_NAME, EVENT_DEFINITION, EVENT_SCHEDULE

FROM information_schema.EVENTS

WHERE EVENT_SCHEMA = 'your_database_name';

6. CONSIDERATIONS FOR USING MYSQL EVENTS

- **Permissions**: Ensure that the user has the EVENT privilege to create, alter, or drop events.
- **Time Zone**: Be mindful of time zones when scheduling events, especially if your application operates across different time zones.

- **Performance**: While events can automate tasks, ensure that the SQL statements in events are optimized to prevent performance degradation.
- **Monitoring**: Regularly monitor event execution and performance to ensure they are functioning as intended.

MySQL Events are a powerful feature that can help automate routine database tasks, improving efficiency and reducing manual intervention. By utilizing events, you can ensure that critical operations are performed on schedule, allowing you to focus on more strategic aspects of database management.

DATA MIGRATION STRATEGIES

Data migration is a crucial process in database management, especially when transitioning from one system to another or upgrading existing infrastructure. It involves moving data between storage types, formats, or systems, and ensuring that data integrity and accessibility are maintained throughout the process. In this section, we will explore various data migration strategies tailored specifically for MySQL environments.

1. UNDERSTANDING DATA MIGRATION

Before diving into specific strategies, it's essential to understand the main objectives of data migration:

- **Data Integrity**: Ensuring that data remains accurate and consistent throughout the migration process.

- **Minimal Downtime**: Reducing the time that applications and users cannot access the database during migration.
- **Compatibility**: Making sure the migrated data is compatible with the new system or database version.
- **Performance**: Maintaining or improving query performance in the new environment.

2. COMMON DATA MIGRATION STRATEGIES

2.1. Big Bang Migration

Big Bang Migration is a strategy where all data is migrated at once during a scheduled downtime. This method is straightforward and can be effective for smaller datasets.

Pros:

- Simple and easy to plan.
- All data is moved in one operation.

Cons:

- Requires significant downtime.
- Higher risk of data loss if issues arise during migration.

Example:

1. Take a backup of the current MySQL database.
2. Shut down the application and database.
3. Migrate all data to the new MySQL instance.
4. Start the new database and bring the application back online.

2.2. Trickle Migration

Trickle Migration involves migrating data incrementally over time. This method allows for ongoing operations while data is being moved, minimizing downtime.

Pros:

- Reduces downtime significantly.
- Lower risk of data loss as migration is gradual.

Cons:

- More complex to implement and manage.
- Requires careful synchronization between source and target systems.

Example:

1. Start by migrating a subset of the data while both systems run in parallel.
2. Regularly sync changes between the old and new systems.
3. Once all data is migrated, switch the application to the new database.

2.3. Hybrid Migration

Hybrid Migration combines elements of both Big Bang and Trickle migration strategies. It involves migrating critical data first (using a Big Bang approach) and then gradually moving less critical data (using a Trickle approach).

Pros:

- Balances the need for immediate access to critical data with a phased approach for less critical data.
- Reduces overall risk by allowing time for testing.

Cons:

- Requires careful planning and execution.
- Complexity increases with multiple migration phases.

Example:

1. Identify critical tables and migrate them first using a Big Bang strategy.
2. Follow up by migrating less critical data incrementally.
3. Ensure proper synchronization during the entire process.

3. PREPARING FOR DATA MIGRATION

Regardless of the strategy chosen, preparation is key to a successful data migration:

3.1. Data Assessment

- Evaluate the current data structure, size, and quality.
- Identify any data inconsistencies or redundancies that need addressing.

3.2. Migration Planning

- Develop a detailed migration plan, including timelines and resource allocation.
- Create a rollback plan in case of migration failures.

3.3. Testing

- Test the migration process with a subset of data before the full migration.
- Validate data integrity and application performance post-migration.

4. POST-MIGRATION ACTIVITIES

Once the migration is complete, several activities should be performed to ensure success:

4.1. Data Validation

- Verify that all data has been accurately migrated.
- Perform checks to ensure data integrity and consistency.

4.2. Performance Tuning

- Analyze query performance on the new system.
- Optimize indexes and configuration settings as needed.

4.3. Monitoring

- Monitor the new database for performance issues or errors.
- Ensure that backup and recovery processes are functioning correctly.

Data migration is a complex yet essential process for maintaining effective database management in MySQL. Choosing the right strategy depends on the specific needs of the organization, the size of the dataset, and the acceptable downtime. By preparing adequately and following best practices, you can ensure a smooth transition to your new database environment.

HANDLING CONCURRENCY ISSUES

Concurrency issues arise when multiple transactions or users attempt to access and modify the same data simultaneously in a database. In MySQL, handling these issues effectively is crucial to maintaining data integrity, consistency, and overall application performance. In this section, we will explore common concurrency problems, their causes, and strategies to handle them in MySQL.

1. UNDERSTANDING CONCURRENCY

Concurrency refers to the ability of a database to allow multiple transactions to occur simultaneously. While this can improve performance and responsiveness, it can also lead to issues such as:

- **Lost Updates**: When two transactions read the same data and then update it, one of the updates may be lost.
- **Dirty Reads**: When a transaction reads uncommitted data from another transaction, leading to potential inconsistencies.

- **Non-Repeatable Reads**: When a transaction reads the same data multiple times and receives different values due to concurrent updates by other transactions.
- **Phantom Reads**: When a transaction reads a set of rows that match a condition and another transaction inserts or deletes rows that affect the results before the first transaction is complete.

2. ISOLATION LEVELS

MySQL supports several transaction isolation levels that define how transactions interact with each other and how concurrency issues are managed. These levels are part of the SQL standard and can be set for each session or globally. The four main isolation levels are:

2.1. Read Uncommitted

- Allows dirty reads.
- Transactions can see uncommitted changes made by other transactions.

2.2. Read Committed

- Prevents dirty reads.
- A transaction can only see changes made by committed transactions.
- Non-repeatable reads can still occur.

2.3. Repeatable Read

- Prevents dirty and non-repeatable reads.

- Ensures that if a transaction reads a row, subsequent reads within the same transaction will return the same values, even if other transactions modify the data.
- Phantom reads can still occur.

2.4. Serializable

- The highest isolation level.
- Prevents dirty reads, non-repeatable reads, and phantom reads by ensuring complete isolation of transactions.
- This level can lead to decreased performance due to increased locking.

Setting Isolation Levels

You can set the isolation level for your session in MySQL using the following command:

SET SESSION TRANSACTION ISOLATION LEVEL <level>;

For example, to set the isolation level to Repeatable Read, you would use:

SET SESSION TRANSACTION ISOLATION LEVEL REPEATABLE READ;

3. LOCKING MECHANISMS

MySQL uses locking mechanisms to handle concurrency and prevent issues:

3.1. Row-Level Locks

- Locks individual rows being modified.
- Allows other transactions to read or modify other rows in the same table.

3.2. Table-Level Locks

- Locks the entire table for reading or writing.
- Can lead to reduced concurrency, as other transactions must wait for the lock to be released.

3.3. Deadlocks

- Occur when two or more transactions are waiting for each other to release locks.
- MySQL automatically detects deadlocks and will terminate one of the transactions to resolve the issue.

4. STRATEGIES TO HANDLE CONCURRENCY ISSUES

4.1. Optimistic Locking

- Assumes that multiple transactions can complete without interfering with each other.
- Before committing, a transaction checks if the data it read has changed. If it has, the transaction is rolled back, and the user is prompted to retry.

4.2. Pessimistic Locking

- Assumes conflicts will occur and locks the data as soon as it is read.
- This prevents other transactions from accessing the locked data until the first transaction is complete.

4.3. Using Transactions

- Always use transactions to group related operations, ensuring that either all changes are committed or none at all.
- Use the BEGIN, COMMIT, and ROLLBACK statements to control transaction boundaries.

Example of a Transaction

START TRANSACTION;

UPDATE accounts SET balance = balance - 100 WHERE account_id = 1;

UPDATE accounts SET balance = balance + 100 WHERE account_id = 2;

COMMIT;

5. MONITORING AND ANALYZING CONCURRENCY ISSUES

Regular monitoring can help identify and resolve concurrency issues:

5.1. Performance Schema

- Use MySQL's Performance Schema to monitor transaction activities, lock waits, and deadlocks.

5.2. Query Logs

- Enable general and slow query logs to analyze how concurrent transactions are impacting performance.

Handling concurrency issues in MySQL is vital for maintaining the integrity and performance of your database. By understanding isolation levels, leveraging locking mechanisms, and implementing effective strategies, you can mitigate the risks associated with concurrent transactions.

UNDERSTANDING ISOLATION LEVELS

Isolation levels are a crucial concept in database management systems (DBMS), including MySQL. They define how transactions interact with each other, particularly when multiple transactions are accessing the same data concurrently. Understanding these levels is essential for managing data consistency, integrity, and performance.

1. WHAT ARE ISOLATION LEVELS?

Isolation levels specify the degree to which the operations in one transaction are isolated from those in other concurrent transactions. The four main isolation levels defined by the SQL standard are:

- **Read Uncommitted**
- **Read Committed**
- **Repeatable Read**
- **Serializable**

Each level provides a different balance between data consistency and system performance.

2. ISOLATION LEVEL DESCRIPTIONS

2.1. Read Uncommitted

- **Description**: This is the lowest isolation level. Transactions can read data that has been modified but not yet committed by other transactions. This means dirty reads are possible.
- **Pros**: Provides the highest level of concurrency and performance.
- **Cons**: Data read may be inconsistent and subject to change, leading to unreliable results.

SET SESSION TRANSACTION ISOLATION LEVEL READ UNCOMMITTED;

2.2. Read Committed

- **Description**: At this level, transactions can only read data that has been committed. This prevents dirty reads but allows non-repeatable reads.
- **Pros**: Reduces the risk of reading uncommitted changes.
- **Cons**: Data may change between reads within the same transaction, leading to inconsistencies.

SET SESSION TRANSACTION ISOLATION LEVEL READ COMMITTED;

2.3. Repeatable Read

- **Description**: This isolation level ensures that if a transaction reads a row, subsequent reads within the same transaction will return the same values, even if other transactions modify the data. It prevents dirty reads and non-repeatable reads but can still experience phantom reads.
- **Pros**: Offers a balance between consistency and concurrency.
- **Cons**: May lead to decreased performance due to increased locking and resource usage.

SET SESSION TRANSACTION ISOLATION LEVEL REPEATABLE READ;

2.4. Serializable

- **Description**: This is the highest isolation level. It ensures complete isolation from other transactions, preventing dirty reads, non-repeatable reads, and phantom reads. All transactions are executed in a way that ensures they appear to be executed serially, one after another.
- **Pros**: Guarantees the highest data consistency.
- **Cons**: Can lead to significant performance degradation due to increased locking and blocking, making it the least concurrent option.

SET SESSION TRANSACTION ISOLATION LEVEL SERIALIZABLE;

3. CHOOSING THE RIGHT ISOLATION LEVEL

When choosing the appropriate isolation level for your application, consider the following factors:

- **Data Consistency Requirements**: If your application demands high data integrity, you may prefer higher isolation levels like Repeatable Read or Serializable.
- **Concurrency Needs**: If your application requires high throughput with many concurrent users, lower isolation levels such as Read Committed or Read Uncommitted may be more suitable.
- **Performance Impact**: Higher isolation levels often incur additional overhead due to locking mechanisms, potentially impacting performance.

4. IMPLEMENTING ISOLATION LEVELS IN MYSQL

You can set the isolation level for a session or globally in MySQL. Here's how to do it for a specific session:

SET SESSION TRANSACTION ISOLATION LEVEL <level>;

To check the current isolation level:

SELECT @@tx_isolation;

To set a global isolation level:

SET GLOBAL TRANSACTION ISOLATION = <level>;

Understanding isolation levels is essential for managing concurrency and ensuring data integrity in MySQL. Each level has its trade-offs between consistency and performance, and the right choice depends on the specific requirements of your application.

DATA WAREHOUSING CONCEPTS

Data warehousing is a critical aspect of modern data management and analytics. It involves the collection, storage, and management of large volumes of data from various sources, enabling organizations to perform complex queries and analysis for decision-making. In this section, we'll explore the fundamental concepts of data warehousing, its architecture, and its importance.

1. WHAT IS A DATA WAREHOUSE?

A **data warehouse** is a centralized repository that stores data from multiple sources, optimized for query and analysis rather than transaction processing. It supports the analytical processes of an organization by consolidating data, allowing for the retrieval of historical data for reporting and analysis.

Key Characteristics of Data Warehouses:

- **Subject-Oriented**: Organized around key subjects or areas of interest (e.g., sales, finance, customer).
- **Integrated**: Combines data from different sources into a cohesive data model.
- **Time-Variant**: Stores historical data, allowing for trend analysis over time.
- **Non-Volatile**: Data is stable and not subject to frequent changes, unlike operational databases.

2. DATA WAREHOUSING ARCHITECTURE

Data warehouses typically follow a multi-tier architecture, which includes:

2.1. Data Source Layer

- **Description**: The layer where data is extracted from various operational systems, external data sources, and other databases. Sources may include CRM systems, ERP systems, and flat files.

2.2. Data Staging Layer

- **Description**: A temporary storage area where raw data is cleaned, transformed, and prepared for loading into the data warehouse. This process is often referred to as ETL (Extract, Transform, Load).

    o **Extract**: Gathering data from source systems.
    o **Transform**: Cleaning and transforming data into a suitable format.
    o **Load**: Storing the transformed data into the data warehouse.

2.3. Data Warehouse Layer

- **Description**: The central repository that stores the processed data. It is optimized for read operations, enabling efficient querying and reporting.

2.4. Presentation Layer

- **Description**: The layer where end-users access and analyze the data. This may include business intelligence tools, dashboards, and reporting systems that provide insights through data visualization.

3. DATA MODELS IN DATA WAREHOUSING

Data warehousing often employs specific data modeling techniques to structure the data effectively. The two most common approaches are:

3.1. Star Schema

- **Description**: A simple design where a central fact table (containing measurable data) is connected to multiple dimension tables (containing descriptive attributes). This schema facilitates easy and efficient querying.

3.2. Snowflake Schema

- **Description**: An extension of the star schema where dimension tables are normalized into multiple related tables. While it reduces data redundancy, it can lead to more complex queries due to additional joins.

4. IMPORTANCE OF DATA WAREHOUSING

Data warehousing plays a vital role in modern organizations by enabling:

- **Improved Decision Making**: By providing a comprehensive view of historical and current data, decision-makers can make informed choices.
- **Enhanced Data Analysis**: Users can perform complex queries and analyses without impacting the performance of operational systems.

- **Increased Efficiency**: Centralizing data allows for better data management and governance, reducing data silos and redundancy.
- **Support for Business Intelligence**: Data warehouses serve as the foundation for business intelligence (BI) solutions, enabling advanced analytics and reporting.

Understanding data warehousing concepts is essential for anyone involved in data management and analysis. A well-designed data warehouse can provide significant insights and drive strategic decisions in an organization.

DISASTER RECOVERY PLANNING

Disaster recovery planning is a crucial aspect of database management, especially for critical systems that require high availability and reliability. In the context of MySQL databases, it involves creating strategies and procedures to protect data and restore database functionality in the event of a disaster, such as hardware failures, data corruption, cyberattacks, or natural disasters. This section will cover the importance of disaster recovery planning, essential components, and best practices.

1. WHAT IS DISASTER RECOVERY PLANNING?

Disaster Recovery Planning (DRP) refers to the processes and procedures that ensure the recovery of IT infrastructure and operations after a disaster. In the realm of databases, it focuses on maintaining data integrity, minimizing downtime, and ensuring business continuity.

Key Goals of Disaster Recovery Planning:

- **Data Protection**: Safeguarding data from loss or corruption.
- **Minimizing Downtime**: Reducing the time it takes to restore services after a disaster.
- **Ensuring Business Continuity**: Maintaining operations and services to minimize impact on users and stakeholders.

2. COMPONENTS OF DISASTER RECOVERY PLANNING

A robust disaster recovery plan for MySQL databases includes several key components:

2.1. Backup Strategies

- **Regular Backups**: Schedule frequent backups (daily, weekly, etc.) of your MySQL databases. Both full and incremental backups should be considered.
- **Backup Types**:

  - **Full Backup**: A complete snapshot of the entire database.
  - **Incremental Backup**: Only backs up the changes made since the last backup.
  - **Differential Backup**: Backs up all changes made since the last full backup.

- **Offsite Storage**: Store backups in a secure offsite location to protect against physical disasters.

2.2. Replication

- **Master-Slave Replication**: Set up replication to maintain a live copy of the database on another server. In the event of a disaster, you can switch to the replica server.
- **Multi-Master Replication**: Allows multiple databases to accept writes, providing redundancy and high availability.

2.3. Recovery Procedures

- **Detailed Recovery Steps**: Document the exact steps to restore data from backups, including commands and tools to be used.
- **Test Recovery Processes**: Regularly perform drills to ensure that the recovery process works as intended and that team members are familiar with the procedures.

2.4. Monitoring and Alerts

- **Set Up Monitoring Tools**: Use monitoring tools to track database performance, backups, and replication status.
- **Alert Systems**: Implement alerting systems to notify the IT team of potential issues before they escalate into disasters.

3. BEST PRACTICES FOR DISASTER RECOVERY PLANNING

3.1. Regularly Review and Update the Plan

- Ensure that the disaster recovery plan is reviewed and updated regularly, especially after significant changes to the database structure or infrastructure.

3.2. Documentation

- Maintain clear and detailed documentation of the disaster recovery plan, including backup schedules, recovery procedures, and contact information for key personnel.

3.3. Training

- Conduct regular training sessions for your IT staff to ensure they are familiar with the disaster recovery plan and can execute it effectively during a crisis.

3.4. Compliance and Regulations

- Ensure that your disaster recovery plan complies with any industry-specific regulations regarding data protection and recovery.

Disaster recovery planning is an essential aspect of managing MySQL databases, enabling organizations to protect their data and maintain operational continuity in the face of unexpected events. By implementing robust backup strategies, replication, and recovery procedures, businesses can minimize the impact of disasters and ensure a swift return to normal operations.

CONCLUSION

As we reach the end of this book, I hope you've gained a solid foundation in MySQL and a clearer understanding of how powerful data management can be when used effectively.

Whether you're a beginner just starting out or a seasoned developer looking to deepen your knowledge, my goal was to guide you through practical, real-world applications of MySQL, drawing from my experiences across different industries.

Throughout these chapters, we've covered everything from setting up databases and writing complex queries to optimizing performance and handling large-scale data.

I shared insights learned over the years working with startups, banks, insurance companies, and the private energy sector, showing how MySQL can be adapted to meet a wide variety of needs.

The flexibility and reliability of this DBMS are what make it such a valuable tool, capable of supporting anything from a small web application to a mission-critical enterprise system.

But the lessons go beyond the technical. MySQL is not just about commands and syntax; it's about solving real-world problems.

It's about designing systems that are efficient, reliable, and scalable. I hope that through this book, you've not only learned how to use MySQL but also developed the mindset needed to approach data management challenges with confidence and creativity.

Learning doesn't stop here.

Technology continues to evolve, and there's always something new to explore. If you ever need a more visual or hands-on approach to any of the topics covered, I invite you to check out my YouTube channel, **4rtisn**, at youtube.com/@4rtisn.

There, you'll find free courses designed to complement this book, offering step-by-step guides and demonstrations to reinforce your learning. Just as this book serves as a deeper companion to those lessons, the channel provides practical examples to bring the concepts we've covered to life.

Together, they form a complete, immersive learning experience to support you on your journey.

As we wrap up, I also want to remind you that success in tech is not just about mastering tools—it's about maintaining a balanced life.

I know firsthand how easy it is to get lost in the world of code and coffee, but it's crucial to find time to disconnect, recharge, and nurture your well-being.

On my Instagram, **@4rtisn**, I share my own efforts to find balance, with hobbies, travel, and moments away from the screen. I'd love for you to follow me there, not just to see what I'm up to, but to join a community of like-minded individuals who understand the importance of balance in a tech-driven world.

Finally, I'd love to hear from you. If you've made it this far, thank you for joining me on this journey through MySQL. Your feedback is invaluable, and I'm always looking to learn how I can improve and help others.

So, I invite you to reach out and send me a message on Instagram at instagram.com/4rtisn. Let me know what you thought of the book, what you enjoyed, and even what could be better. I look forward to hearing your thoughts and continuing the conversation.

Thank you, and happy coding!

www.ingramcontent.com/pod-product-compliance
Lightning Source LLC
LaVergne TN
LVHW041208050326
832903LV00021B/534